Confronting
The
Bottle

Emma Bushen

&

Joanne Haywood

Yellow Rose Publishing Ltd

First published in United Kingdom in 2014 by

Yellow Rose Publishing Ltd

A CIP catalogue record for this title is available from the British Library

ISBN 978-0-9574098-1-1

Printed and bound by Lightning Source UK Ltd

Disclaimer

We have tried to recreate events, locales and conversations from Emma's memories of them. In order to maintain their anonymity in some instances the names of individuals have changed and some identifying characteristics.

Joanne Haywood

Co-Writer

www.facebook.com/GirlFridayStoke

Blog: www.girlfridaystoke.wordpress.com

Email: girlfridaystoke@gmail.com

In Loving Memory

Tony Boyd

5.5.1968 – 2.8.2014

Who sadly lost his battle with the illness.

Acknowledgements

The last three years in sobriety have been the most special of my life so far. Sobriety taught me a different way to live, and most importantly feel inside.

I know I wouldn't even have reached Sobriety without the love and support of my husband James, I am so lucky to have someone who chose to believe in me, and love me enough to help me find the answer, even after I had totally destroyed him inside. I love him with all my heart and will be forever thankful to him.

I am so grateful to still have the title "Mum" after the way I treated and hurt my three children. I love all of them so much, and I'm so proud today of the new relationships we have all re-built together. From the bottom of my heart I thank them for the love they fill my heart with every day.

Without my nans belief in me growing up as a child and right into adulthood, my behaviour could have been even worse than it was. I let her down and also hurt her many times, I always want her to know she will be one of the most important people in my life.

Recovery was undoubtedly one of the darkest places I've ever been. Life was scary and I felt like an alien on a new planet.

I was so lucky to have by my side Alison, my best friend throughout my life but especially through recovery. Alison and her husband Kelly helped me and James re-build our relationship. I know we wouldn't have survived without them, they will always be part of our family.

Jenny and Rich are two of the kindest people I've ever met. I'm so sorry for all the years of pain I caused to their whole family, and will also be forever grateful for their support during my recovery. I appreciate and love them both so much and they are the most loving grandparents to my children, I feel so lucky to have them in my life.

Along my journey through recovery my Facebook page "Confronting Life Without the Bottle" I made more friends than I've ever had in my life, from all over the world the support I've received has been amazing. The page not only helps others but it has also helped me on my own bad days. I feel I have a place to share my experiences and advice, this played a massive part in my recovery. Thank you so much to every one of you for all the love and support over the years.

My co-writer Jo Haywood has become a true friend. The dedication she has put into all the writing from my scribbled notes has blown me away! She is such a talented writer and I feel privileged to have had her help along this incredible journey.

To Nicola Simpson, my publisher for having that first faith in my story, and for teaching me so much about life. It's been a total dream to work with someone I have so much respect for personally.

Sally has recently joined us as our proof-reader, she's been an amazing member of the team, and so supportive, it's been a pleasure getting to know her.

I was so surprised when my old school friend Kelly contacted me about a year in to my recovery to offer her support and a photo shoot for my front cover. I absolutely loved the whole experience and am delighted with the results. She's fantastic and I really appreciate her thinking of me and my family.

All the organisations agencies and charities that helped our family were so kind, thank you.

To the refuge for giving me and my family that new start, I'm so sorry I wasted the opportunity, everyone's friendship and advice will always stay with me.

To our social worker, Peter, for the care he gave to me and my family, he went beyond the call of duty in my opinion and I will appreciate what he did forever.

To Richard Chambers from The Kenward Trust for providing the quote for the cover of this book. It's an honour from someone who does so much to help people make it into recovery.

An extra special thank you to my husband James who has worked so hard to create the front cover for me, he wasn't fazed by any of our requests or alterations, thanks you.

Finally to the doctor that gave me that final piece of advice that led me on to my recovery. She started the awakening inside me, by forcing me to face it all, and most importantly accepting it.

I now wake up every day feeling lucky and happy.

To everyone that helped me make it to here, thank you so, so much

Emma xx

Would you like to join me on Facebook?

Search for: Confronting Life Without the Bottle

Foreword

Today I feel loved. I have never felt that before, or allowed myself to.

I feel so much more responsible now as a wife and as a mother. When I look back on some of the things I did it makes me feel sick, but I feel so lucky to have found the answer to all the pain.

People trust and respect me now, and I would never want to lose that again.

The bond I have with my children and family has never been stronger, and I appreciate every day that we spend together.

I have written my story as honestly as I can, with the intention of giving others the hope I lacked for the longest time. During those times, I did some things I'm not proud of, I allowed myself to be taken advantage of, and I found myself at a point lower than I believed possible.

It took every ounce of strength my family and I had, to turn my life around, but now we live with love and hope every day.

This is my story.

Emma x

Chapter 1

To anyone looking at me as a child, I must have seemed happy. In truth, for as long as I can remember, I was hiding behind a smile.

I hated my body and I don't ever remember feeling comfortable.

Although I wouldn't notice it physically until my teenage years; I was born with a curved spine. It wasn't, and still isn't hugely noticeable, but when I bent over and the other kids at school saw it they teased and called me names. Silly things like: "hunchback," or "penguin." Never full bullying, but enough to make a girl with insecurities feel a little bit worse about herself.

I can't remember a time when I wasn't insecure or trying to fit in but I had a happy childhood and wanted for nothing. We had a happy home and when I was much younger we would have family parties where grandparents, aunts, uncles and cousins would all get together, I loved these times.

A few months after my Grandads passing I remember there was a big family argument. It wasn't long before we stopped seeing the extended family as much and I missed them terribly.

I've always found it hard to form bonds with people. When I was younger I would get nervous, stammer and stutter. One of the reasons I used to drink so much was to give myself the confidence I felt I needed; especially if I was meeting new people for the first time. Looking back, I've wondered whether these arguments might give a little insight into that: I was scared to let people in or allow them to get close as I was worried they'd be taken away from me, and because I never knew the reason for the big argument within our family I wondered if I was to blame.

As well as stammering, I would also blush easily and while other children seemed to have natural confidence, I felt awkward.

It wasn't until I was a teenager that I began to drink and found an answer to my problems. Looking back, it seems easy to suggest that I should have got, or been given, some help to deal with my anxiety, but I didn't understand why I felt the way I did. Nobody offered to help or could see inside my head, and so I struggled.

I felt angry with everyone, and just wanted to scream for help. I know now that most teenagers feel this way, but I felt so alone, that my only option was to push the boundaries as much as I could.

I put my parents through hell by rebelling against them at every opportunity.

If there was a rule in place, I would find a way to break it. From playing truant, to stealing, smoking and drinking; I pushed my family to their limits.

Of course, drinking would become the major focus and I can still remember the first time I got drunk. Like many other teenage girls, myself and a group of friends thought it would be great to put our money together and buy some alcohol. We found someone to buy us the strongest and most "grown up" drink we could find and, full of giggles, we headed to my house to drink it. Unlike my friends, I wasn't scared of being caught and I didn't care about getting into trouble with my parents so my house was the best option.

While my friends were relatively sensible with the whisky and made sure they didn't drink too much, I got completely paralytic and ended up throwing up all over the sofa my parents had just bought.

The sofa was not only brand new but was made from material and was now stained. My parents were, of course, furious and banned me from the family holiday we were due to go on, and instead made me stay with my Nan. To this day, Nan and I are still close. Nan has always been there for me and she's the only family member I still have a relationship with.

In spite of this I still hadn't finished pushing their boundaries, and at the age of seventeen I delivered the news that I was pregnant. They were so angry that they threw me out and I moved in with my (then) boyfriend's parents.

As much as I'd pushed them in the past, and as much as we'd argued, I was devastated by the rejection especially when I needed them most. Deep down, I know that they were disappointed in me and looking back I think that this was their way of trying to get me to change my mind about keeping the baby but I was stubborn and my mind was made up. With, or without them; I was having the baby.

Just as I'm sure my parents had expected, the relationship didn't last, and after a few months I was allowed to go back home.

I gave birth to Luke in August 1998, and for a while everything seemed to be working out. Luke was a lovely baby, and for a time he brought me and my mum back together again; she was a huge help and made a lovely nanny.

When Luke was six months old, I was offered a council flat. The area was really nice and it gave us a fresh start; I was so excited about the life we would build for ourselves and our future seemed bright.

We were happy at first and settled in well, but a month later I noticed that Luke wasn't himself. He was being sick and his temperature was high; I was worried and rushed him to the doctor. The doctor quickly referred us to the hospital. As I paced and worried, they carried out tests and finally confirmed the news that all parents dread - Luke had Meningitis!

We were rushed under a police escort to Guys Hospital in London, and Luke was admitted to intensive care. The doctors were very open with me about his chances and told me he was very poorly and that he might not survive the illness. It was an awful time for all of us, and poor Luke had to endure: tests, treatments, needles and, worst of all, injections into his skull as the veins in his body weren't functioning properly.

I was terrified I would lose him and was crying hysterically. Although I didn't want to leave Luke's side, the doctors told me that I had to wait outside while they treated him. I could only stand on the other side of the door shaking with fear as I heard my tiny boy screaming in pain.

My mum had come with me and never left my side, we waited together and eventually she told me to take a break and go for a cup of tea. She must have known that I was on the verge of breaking down completely and told me that she would wait outside for any news and shout for me if I was needed.

I took some persuading but I could see that she was right, so I went to the drinks machine and got a cup of tea. I couldn't stay away for too long though so I took my hot drink and headed back to the corridor outside the Paediatric Intensive Care Unit. When I returned, I realised that she had gone inside to hold Luke and comfort him as he recovered.

It must have been awful for her to go in and see him like that, but I appreciated her so much for doing it.

A little while later, Luke seemed to brighten and like the fighter he was, and still is, he started to gain some strength and pull himself out of the fever.

Not only did he escape with no side effects at all, but within a week he was able to leave intensive care and go to a standard children's ward. Another short week later, he was allowed to come home. I was overjoyed and made the most of my time with him. His time in hospital had been so hard on him, and between me, my mum and dad and his father's side of the family we made sure he was spoiled rotten. We felt so lucky and grateful to have him with us.

It was about a month before things started to get back to normal. Luke was well enough for me to start going out with him again and, although I felt a little nervous, I arranged to meet my mum in town.

I didn't drive, so I planned to get the bus and have some lunch with her.

Public transport was terrible from my house. There was only a bus every hour so I made sure I was early and had collapsed my pushchair ready to get on. This was no easy task, especially as I had to hold Luke at the same time.

When the bus pulled up, the driver said I couldn't get on as there wasn't enough room for the pushchair even though I had it folded and was ready. I couldn't believe what he was telling me; especially as the bus was half-empty and had a designated space for pushchairs. I pointed at the space, nearly in tears at his attitude, and he told me that he had to keep that space free in case somebody elderly or disabled needed to get on.

By that point I was furious and holding a heavy pushchair and a screaming baby, so I told him in no uncertain terms what I thought of him and his attitude.

It didn't seem to matter to him or change his mind and I realised I wasn't going to be able to meet my mum as planned, so I set about huffily putting my pram back together. A girl my age had just got off the bus and she smiled kindly at me. She offered to give me a hand and told me not to worry about the miserable bus driver.

That made me smile, so I thanked her and introduced myself. She told me her name was Alison and asked how old Luke was. She told me she had a little boy a year older. Her son was called Reece and, like me, she'd had him very young.

As we started to walk together we realised that we lived in the same street.

By the time we got to the end of our road, a friendship had been born. We had loads in common: friends, situations and a silly sense of humour, the more we talked the more I liked her.

I'd never felt quite as at ease with a stranger as I did with Alison, and I told her that if she was ever at a loose end she should come over. That night I was surprised and overjoyed to find her on my doorstep and from that night onwards we saw each other most days.

Reece and Luke would happily play together as we chatted. We would often take the children to the park near our home where they loved to run around on the grass.

Alison and I also used to take the children into The Bull Inn. The Bull was a family pub with a beer garden where the kids could play and we would sit with a coke while the children enjoyed themselves in the garden. If it was a nice day, we'd have a lager each, I do wonder if it was the start of the journey I was to go on.

When we could get babysitters, the two of us would also go

for nights out in the town. Neither of us had much money so we'd spend our nights trying to get people to buy us drinks. On the occasions that we managed to get quite a few drinks bought for us, I started to notice a change in me.

I'm ashamed of it now but sometimes I would bite her. She would always tell me the next day and although I never hurt her or left a mark on her arm, we would laugh it off at the time as a "funny thing drunk Emma does," it wasn't funny and I now realise it was just one more symptom of how much the drink changed me as a person.

As well as Alison, I also had my friend Penny who I enjoyed drinking with. Her brother Tim was my sister's boyfriend and as they were settled down Penny and I would go out without them. When I went out with Penny though we would both drink heavily and I would pay for it the next day, feeling really ill.

I suppose the bad hangovers should have stopped me drinking so much, but I told myself that I deserved to have a little fun after having Luke so young and missing out on what my friends had been doing. I was convinced that I was young and single, and deserved to be able to let my hair down.

One night Penny and I went out for the night to a local nightclub called "Chicago's." It had a great atmosphere and we loved the music. I've always loved the cheesy seventies and eighties music and still do. Chicago's played a great selection of those tunes and as soon as I stepped inside I was in a party mood. We always had a great time and it was one place that I always looked forward to going.

I can still remember exactly what I was wearing that night. Although I had a slim figure, I'd covered up because I suffered badly with eczema and it had covered my legs. I'd normally wear a dress when we went out but this night I wore silk trousers and a top. In spite of this, with a few drinks inside me, I felt full of confidence and as the night wore on, my confidence grew.

Penny was staying at my house, and we'd agreed if we were separated, we'd meet up later to go home together. We'd done the same thing before and it had worked perfectly.

I felt lucky that night; I skipped a few meals and saved the money so I had lots to spend on my great night out. I did that a lot when I was younger, and my slim figure was thanks in part to the meals I missed. It never occurred to me that I was getting so drunk because I wasn't eating properly and on that particular night I got really drunk.

My memories in the club are a little blurred. But what happened to me later on that night will haunt me forever.

Chicago's was full, I'd had a lot to drink and was feeling really positive and I got talking to a group of guys.

Among the group was a guy called Neil. He seemed really nice and brought me loads of drinks while we chatted. Looking back, I shouldn't have carried on drinking as I'd had enough already but being me I carried on drinking and he carried on buying.

Towards the end of the night, Neil asked me to go back to where he stayed with him and his friends. Because of the amount I'd drunk, and because I was excited I forgot all about Penny and left the club. Poor Penny had nowhere to sleep and can't have known where I was but at the time I was so carried away with what I was doing and with the amount I'd had to drink that I forgot to tell her I was leaving or make sure she was all right. I remember feeling awful about it the next morning.

The rest of the night will stay with me for the rest of my life.

Although we'd gone back to his place with a group, Neil and I broke off and went back to his room. We started kissing and he started to undress me. He took my trousers off and as he saw the eczema on my legs he changed immediately. He told me it was disgusting and told me to turn over onto my front so that he couldn't see it any more

The change in him and the cruelty he used, started to sober me up and I told him that I wanted to stop what we were doing. He didn't stop, and that night Neil raped me.

I don't want to dwell on what happened and although it's something that I've never dealt with or really come to terms with, it's not the focus of this story.

When I got home I contacted the police to tell them what had happened but it was my word against his and there wasn't any evidence to show that I hadn't consented to sleeping with him, so my complaint never went any further. It left me distraught for a very long time.

Chapter 2

It took me a long time to recover from that night and for at least six months I didn't go out at all. I shut myself off to the world and only spent time with Luke, my family and of course, my closest friend Alison.

Alison was my rock, and still is. We grew closer over those six months and she would always be a shoulder to cry on or have time to listen to me. She would always try to cheer me up and make me smile.

Although I got a lot of support from my family, and a lot of help with Luke, I couldn't really talk to them about what happened. We've never been the kind of family who share feelings and this would be no exception. It's not a criticism of them; simply the way they are, and as a result I think that it was thanks to Alison that I gained the confidence to restart my life.

I enrolled Luke into the local playschool and he started to settle in well. The playschool was next door to the Bull Inn and Alison and I would do the "school run" together often taking the children into the pub to play on our way home. We never went in to get drunk; we just wanted to be out and about and enjoyed our afternoons together.

We sat in the garden while Luke and Reece played, and as we were becoming regulars Alison and I got to know the staff very well.

Les ran the pub and had a huge personality. He would make

us laugh, and most of all, make us feel welcome. He was famous in our little local town as the landlord who stood behind the bar with his microphone. He'd shout or announce little things like who'd just walked in and make us all fall about laughing. He was short with curly hair and was always wearing a football t-shirt.

While Les would run the bar, his wife Dawn ran the food side of things. She was lovely too, but because she worked in the kitchen we didn't see as much of her.

Jenny also worked behind the bar. She was lovely and I remember liking her straight away. She had stunning blue eyes that seemed like they were smiling, short dark hair and always looked immaculate. She was attractive and, at all times, dressed very elegantly. In short, she was the perfect person to work behind a bar, and was great at welcoming customers and putting them at ease.

She was happy, friendly and made a huge fuss of the kids – who loved her in return.

One afternoon there was a new man behind the bar. I quickly found out that his name was James and commented to Jenny "Cor, he's nice." Jenny laughed and told me that she knew just how nice he was; he was her son.

Alison said she'd been to school with him and thought he was good looking too.

The next time we went in, it was lunchtime and we'd just popped in for a quick drink while the kids had a play on the swings in the garden. James came straight up and spoke to me. I nearly died on the spot when I found out that Jenny had spilled the beans about me liking him and I went bright red.

I can also remember that I was wearing a silly hairpiece which was all the rage at the time and I couldn't believe that I hadn't made more of an effort.

James didn't seem to mind though, and he asked if I would go on a date with him. As shy as I was, James seemed really confident and outgoing. We didn't know a thing about each other so the conversation was a little awkward, but I really liked him.

Wanting to say yes and actually saying yes were two different things entirely, and I started to giggle out of nerves. I finally managed to tell him yes. We arranged to meet the following night in the pub where they had karaoke. After that, I took my drink outside, telling Alison that I couldn't believe my luck.

Later, James kept walking past where we were sitting. He was just doing his job but I started to feel really self-conscious. I was getting butterflies in my stomach and starting to have a really good feeling about him, I liked the way he was with the customers; he was so nice.

We walked through the bar to leave and Alison took it upon herself to call out "Bye James," as loud as she could. I was so embarrassed but somehow managed to say bye to him too. When he smiled and said bye my heart did a somersault while my cheeks turned very red.

I was still feeling very raw after what had happened after my night out at Chicago's so I asked Alison and our neighbour Lyn to come with us on my date. I'd told James I was bringing them with me so he was going to bring a friend too.

As well as feeling anxious I was hugely excited and started to make plans. I arranged for my mum to look after Luke overnight. I was really excited as I started to get ready.

The Bull held a Karaoke night once a week; it was popular so a lot busier than usual when we arrived.

I'd had a few drinks before we left the house to steady my nerves and give me a little more confidence, but as we walked in I started to get a little panicked and still didn't feel that I was ready to go over to him, so I sat with the girls at a table near him and his friend Lee.

We'd been there for a while drinking steadily when James got up to sing. He was amazingly good, and I would find out later just how important music was to him.

On the way back to his table he came over to me and jokingly asked: "So are you going to talk to me tonight or not?" The girls got up to sing and James and I were alone for a little while. We chatted and he leaned in to kiss me. I was so happy.

We spent the rest of the night chatting and when the Karaoke finished, James walked me home. I decided to be honest with him and tell him straight away about the rape. I'm sure that it must have been a lot for him to take in on a first date, but I just wanted us to get to know each other and I wanted to be honest. Looking back, I'd probably had a little bit more to drink than I intended, so I said more than I meant to.

He took the revelation really well though, telling me that he would be as patient with me as I needed him to be. Then we kissed again and I went inside.

I must have slept with a smile on my face, and I was still on cloud nine when mum brought Luke home the next morning. She could see how happy I was and was really pleased and hoped things worked out for us.

Later that afternoon I got a text from James saying that he'd had a great time and asked if I'd like to see him again. He didn't need to ask twice and we arranged to meet the following night.

As I didn't have a babysitter this time, I took Luke with me and we met at the pub again. We didn't stay late as we had Luke with us and, in any case, the pub didn't allow children after nine. James and Luke hit it off too with James showering Luke with attention and making a real fuss of him. I loved seeing the two of them together and straight away they seemed like a little double act.

After about a month, James and I decided to take Luke to the seaside for Easter Sunday. Luke was about two years old and we knew he'd love the beach at Leysdown on Sea – but we didn't count on him scoffing his way through tons of Easter eggs and being sick all over the car!

We'd arranged to meet James' mum and dad there too. Of course, I knew Jenny from The Bull, but meeting his dad Rich was a little daunting. I needn't have been worried though, as Rich was lovely to us both and Luke took to him straight away as well.

They'd brought the family dog, Sally, with them. Luke had us all in fits of laughter all day as he couldn't quite pronounce Sally and kept shouting: "Sellin" to her.

We had a fantastic day and finished it off with a fish and chip supper for everyone.

Over the next few months, Luke and I got to know James' whole family. They made just as much of a fuss of him as James did. I loved the way that Jenny and Rich treated Luke as though he was their own grandson. Luke would stay at their house and we would all go out on daytrips together. It wasn't just James' parents though, his entire family were very close and they all welcomed Luke and I and made us feel part of the family.

After our fun at the seaside, Luke and I were invited to a proper "family do" which was a joint christening for two babies in the family. I felt hugely honoured to be considered part of the family and to be invited to the church and the party, Luke and I wore our best clothes.

They were holding the party after the Christening at The Bull

Inn, I immediately felt at home, both there and with the huge family who made us feel like we belonged.

Because he knew The Bull so well, Luke was happily playing in the playground while James introduced me around the family. The play area had a swing, climbing frame and a tubular twisty slide, Luke was running around with the other children when I heard a scream.

Every mother knows her own child's cry and the sound knocked me sick. I excused myself and ran outside to see what was going on and found Luke screaming hysterically.

The other children helped him to tell me that it had been his turn on the slide when he went a little fast and slipped off half way down. He'd gone head first as he fell and landed flat on his face.

Luckily, the floor of the play area was covered in wood chippings so he had a soft landing, but by this point he was rubbing at his nose and crying really hard.

James was by my side as we checked Luke over and realised he had a piece of wood chip lodged inside his nose.

Luke tried to get it out before I got to him but had managed to wedge it up there and it was now stuck. As he clawed at himself to get it out, his poor nose started to bleed from the sharp edges and there was no way we could get it out.

Finally, with the family wishing us well and telling us to keep in touch with them, James took us up to the local Accident and Emergency department to get him seen to. They managed to get it dislodged and let us go home with a very sore and shaken little boy.

* * *

I'd told James from the beginning that I had a weekend break booked with Alison, and although I was really looking forward to it, I wished he could come with me. My mum and dad had paid for the break at Butlins for my 21st birthday and Alison and I were really excited.

James and I had been together for six weeks, and we were already inseparable so leaving him was hard. But I was sure Alison and I would have a good time. Our second night at Butlins we went to the club on site and got drunk, dancing and having a great time. At the end of the evening, we sang 'Girls Just Want to Have Fun' on the Karaoke and made a video of our singing. At the end of the song, I went right up to the camera and said "I love you James."

At the time, I just put it down to the drinking, but when I started to really think about it the next day I realised I did love him. I'd missed him so much and he made me really happy; I'd never felt this way about anyone before.

As part of my birthday present my dad had offered to pick us up from the Butlins camp in Bognor Regis. The day we were due to go home was actually my 21st birthday and so when he arrived, my dad stayed and had a drink with us before we left, and I was desperate for a smoke.

Despite all the boundaries I'd broken with my parents I'd never smoked in front of him before but it suddenly hit me that I was 21 and I remember saying,

"Right Dad, this is it, I'm 21 today and I'm old enough to smoke in front of you now."

Then I just lit up a cigarette right in front of him. I was expecting him to shout at me, but he just laughed and shook his head. I don't think anything I did shocked him anymore.

As it was my birthday, mum and dad had invited Luke and I to theirs for a Chinese takeaway and we'd arranged that they would meet James for the first time.

I couldn't wait to get home; I was so excited to see James

again. I rushed home, got changed and walked down to The Bull were we'd arranged to meet.

As I was going to meet him, I felt nervous and excited just as I had on our first date – and I knew it was because I was going to tell him that I loved him.

When I saw James, I gave him the biggest cuddle and as we sat down I told him how much I'd missed him. I looked right into his eyes, I felt totally comfortable with him, and I wanted to tell him how I was feeling inside.

"James" I said, "while I was away I missed you so much!"

"Well, you know it's that irresistible charm of mine!" he cheekily smiled at me.

I felt so happy, like I had the perfect birthday present.

"No" I said "It was more than that... I actually think I'm falling in love with you!" my heart was pounding.

There, I'd said it and we both fell quiet a second, taking in my words.

James picked up my hand and squeezed it.

"Well!" he said, "I think I can say that I'm feeling it too Emma, hearing you say it first, I've got no excuses now have I?" he smiled putting his arm around me.

"I love you too; I couldn't be happier right now" and he kissed the top of my head.

That night, the three of us went to my mum and dad's for my little birthday party and it was lovely. Luke always had a nice time with them and they really liked James too, so I was absolutely thrilled. After three months, James was spending nearly every night with us and we decided to live together. When he moved in with us, I was so happy; I felt like I had found my soul mate.

Chapter 3

James' parents were really supportive and helped with the move, before we knew it we were a family of three. Because James and Luke had always got on so well, I didn't anticipate any problem with James settling in; although, of course, we'd laid down some ground rules about what James' responsibilities were towards Luke.

James had been living with us for a few days when Alison had come around to see us. James and Alison had always got on really well and I loved the fact that these two people who were so important to me were good friends themselves.

I was in the kitchen talking on the phone whilst James, Alison and Luke were all in the front room when all of a sudden I heard raised voices and Luke crying. I ran in to see what was going on and found James telling Luke off.

James had never raised his voice to Luke before and I was absolutely horrified. I yelled at James and told him to leave. He protested and was trying to tell me why he was shouting at Luke, but I wasn't listening and just told him to get out.

When he'd gone and I'd calmed down enough to listen, Alison told me what had actually happened.

Luke, without any warning, had thrown a glass at James. Luke had never done anything like that before and I was shocked and upset. Then it dawned on me that I'd just thrown James out of his new home and I couldn't believe how quickly things had got out of control.

I ran to the window and luckily James was still walking down the road. He looked so upset that I felt horribly guilty; I banged on the window as loud and hard as I could to get his attention and begged him to come back.

I apologised to James and asked him to give me some time to talk to Luke on my own. The attack was completely out of character for him, and I was desperate to try to see things from his perspective. I asked Luke what he'd done and why he'd done it and he got really upset which just made me feel worse. All the same, what he'd done was very dangerous and I had to tell him. I told him that someone could be hurt by him throwing and that he mustn't do it again. I said he should come to me if he felt upset or angry so that we could try to work something out together. Then I told him that I loved him and would always love him and we had a hug.

Unfortunately, this wasn't the only time Luke struggled to accept James and a few days later James got up for work only to find that Luke had done a poo in his shoes! He'd also taken a bite out of the pork pie James had bought ready for his lunch at work!

From Luke's point of view, the nice man who he saw occasionally in his house and when we went out was not only there all the time now, but he was also taking up some of my time. I can understand how that must have been very disruptive to his little routine and it's no wonder he tried to push some boundaries to get my attention and to see what he could get away with.

For his part, James was amazing with Luke. If anything, the naughty incidents seemed to make James more determined that he and Luke would be friends, James spent as much time with Luke as he could encouraging him to get involved in music.

I remember James trying to teach Luke how to play the

guitar. Of course, music is James' passion and because Luke didn't share the passion to the same extent the two of them bickered like little old men the whole time. They were both highly strung but their little debates over whose technique was best had me in fits of laughter.

Eventually Luke cracked. James had won him over and our home turned into somewhere warm, loud and full of fun with Luke always laughing at funny things James was doing and James and I laughing at Luke.

As well as enjoying time together, James and I settled into a weekend routine where we had fun and partied hard.

We always made sure that we took Luke out for a treat on Friday night before bedtime. James would finish work at five and we'd take Luke out for a McDonalds or down to The Bull for his tea and a few drinks for us.

Once we'd got Luke into bed then our parties would start. I'd stay at home and make sure Luke was okay in bed while James went on a beer run. Often we'd have friends round and because we didn't have much money, James would try to find a good deal on beer. One night he came back from the shop with a bottle of vodka. I'd never tried vodka before but found, straight away, that I loved it.

As well as going down like water, I felt different on the vodka than I had on beer or cider. I felt really happy and confident, as though I could do anything. I felt almost empowered and knew I could get used to feeling like this.

Our parties started turning into a regular thing and we'd all get drunk and a little silly. I remember one night when James and all his mates tried on my clothes for a laugh. We managed to get pictures and spent the next night laughing at them all.

Although we'd often see friends on a Friday night, on

Saturday they'd be at home having an easier night but I was enjoying the partying, so I soon started asking James to make sure he brought enough for me to have a drink on Saturday night too.

Come Sunday I'd feel really rough: tired and drained but not enough to ring any alarm bells.

Although we always had a great time and we all enjoyed it, one night I was really rude to one of James' friends while I was drunk. I couldn't remember anything and when James told me about it the next day I was horrified. I text his friend to apologise and he graciously accepted. I've mentioned before that music is hugely important to James and is a big part of his life. Back then, James was in a band called "Bag of Nails" with his brother Josh, and their two friends; Conner and Mick. James played the guitar and they had a lot of local gigs.

When we first got together I'd go to the gigs with James and the boys. Although their music really wasn't my thing and I'd rather listen to love songs or disco, I did enjoy being the "guitarist's girlfriend." I'd always have a really good time at the gigs and the drink was always flowing as they performed in pubs and clubs.

Over the years, I've lost count of the number of gigs I've ruined for James by drinking too much. With the confidence the booze gave me, I thought I was hilariously funny as I'd be as loud and vulgar as I wanted. I was regularly rude to James' friends or other people at the gigs and felt untouchable as I was drunk. It didn't matter how much I promised myself I'd behave, I ended up making a show of myself and then crying or arguing with James because I'd broken my resolve.

As well as playing music, James loves listening to music and especially seeing music live. One of his favourite bands is 'The Who' and, for his birthday that year, his friends took him to see a tribute band.

I'd asked Jenny to come around and keep me and Luke company and she brought us a few bottles of wine. Jenny and I have always got on well and we had a really nice night. As it got later I was looking forward to James coming home so I could hear all about the band.

At about eleven o'clock James called to say that he was going back to his brothers after the gig for some drinks and that he was going to stay there overnight. I'm sure that in his head it was sensible as he wouldn't wake me or Luke up when he came in, but I saw red.

I went mad and starting shouting at him, "You promised me you were coming home!"

I realise now I was jealous and couldn't stand the idea of him being out without me. We ended up having an argument on the phone and I made him come home.

This wasn't the first time I'd flown into a rage about him being with his mates and reflecting on it now it really makes me cringe. James never gave me any reason to think he was anything other than devoted to Luke and I. He didn't deserve to have me strangling him emotionally. I was acting like a jealous child but I couldn't see it at the time.

There were times when I'd yell at him in public for stupid things and for talking to his friends. What I didn't realise is that I was making us a target for gossip and people were starting to make judgements about us and about me.

When he got home that night, Jenny left us to it, and as soon as she'd gone we ended up having a huge argument. We were shouting so much that we disturbed the neighbours downstairs and I shouted at them to call the police.

The police turned up and arrested James, leaving me to calm down and sober up. I knew I'd behaved really badly and I also now know that if I hadn't been drunk I wouldn't have been so paranoid about him being out.

He came home a few hours later, also sober and calm, and we managed to sort things out between us. But that wouldn't be the last of our huge rows; they were just getting started.

We had a few months of calm and carried on with our weekend parties, and then one week James arranged to go out to the pub to meet his best mate, Kyle. They hadn't seen each other for a while and, as lads tend to do, they got really drunk.

I stayed at home with Luke and by the time James came home to me, I was also really drunk. I was furious with him, although I didn't really have a reason to be. As soon as he came home I flipped.

I started screaming at him and I attacked him; flying at him clawing and hitting out at him. James was so shocked that he left and went to his mum and dad's.

After a little while James came back with Jenny in tow. She was furious with me for lashing out at him, but in the mood I was in, having her there and shouting at me only made me angrier. When the two of them walked in, I turned on Jenny too and James had to hold me back to stop me clawing at her too.

Neither of them had ever seen me like this. In fact I'd never been like this before – and they both left shocked and scared.

The next day I woke up sober and full of regrets. I couldn't believe what I'd done.

At first all of the memories were blurred and a little hazy but as they started to become more lucid I started to feel worse. It's a very frightening thing to wake up with the memories of the night before but being powerless to change them. This was worse than any hangover headache because I felt so ashamed of myself. The feelings just kept rolling over me like a wave and becoming more and more upsetting until I couldn't take it any longer.

Shaking, I went into the kitchen and lit a cigarette. I couldn't think straight, and at the back of my mind was the horrible feeling that I might have ruined things with James. Suddenly I became hysterical and desperate.

I loved him so much; almost obsessively. I'd never felt like that about any relationship I'd been in before and I think it was because of the bond we shared but also because of the bond James had with Luke. We fit perfectly into each other's lives, we had to stay together.

Because of the love I felt for him, I thought I was justified in the way I behaved. It never seemed like I was being possessive at the time. I was just keeping my family together and because of that I was never able to admit how controlling my behaviour towards him was.

I couldn't live without him and I had to make this right. I should have been thinking about the changes I needed to make and what I had done wrong but what I decided to do instead was to find a solution to make him forget about what I'd done.

Eventually I rang his phone. He answered straight away but his voice was cold, "Emma, I've got nothing to say to you. Just go away."

Of course, I couldn't and wouldn't do that so I started to plead with him,

"Please babe, I just want one chance to try and put this right and prove to you how sorry I am."

He agreed to come to the flat to talk but I could tell from the tone of his voice that he was still appalled by what had happened.

We arranged for him to come over that evening after I'd put Luke to bed. I knew I had to be ready for him and to make things better so that afternoon I went to town and bought a ring. I wasn't ready to let my family go without a fight, and so I decided to ask James to be my husband.

Later I put Luke to bed and nervously waited. Despite being so young, Luke knew that something wasn't right. He'd been asking all day where James was and I told him that he'd gone to see Jenny and Rich but would be back in the morning. He'd been upset all day and I know he must have been able to sense the atmosphere and the tension in the flat.

He was unsettled when I put him to bed, and when the doorbell rang, he jumped straight out of bed to run to the door. James was as pleased to see Luke as Luke was to see him and before we started to talk, he went in with Luke to tuck him into bed. Luke had a cuddle and his dummies. He always had two dummies: one for his mouth and one for his hand. He called them his "two's" and so did everyone else – and he couldn't sleep without them.

Having James back helped him to settle down and a few minutes later James came into the kitchen where I was waiting for him.

My heart was pounding and I couldn't cope with all the emotion I was feeling knowing what I was about to do and say, so I burst into tears. James had seen me cry so many times during our arguments that this time he wasn't interested. I could see that the only way I was going to salvage our relationship was to talk; and fast!

I told him that although I couldn't remember a lot from the night before I felt awful about what I'd done. I told him that I'd do anything to make it up to him and his mum. I hated the fact that she'd seen me like that and I felt so shocked and angry with myself for acting the way that I did.

I explained to him how much Luke and I loved him and needed him and I begged him not to give up on us.

Then I grabbed the ring box out of my bag. I was embarrassed and nervous and didn't trust my voice to actually ask him to marry me. In a fit of emotion I threw the box over to him, I was unable to look him in the eye.

He caught the box and opened it. Then he looked me in the eye and said; "how does this change anything?"

Then I tearfully explained that the ring was my promise to change. I would sort myself out. I would do anything he asked and anything he wanted because I couldn't live without him. By this point, I was crying so hard, down on my knees pleading with him to forgive me and to accept the ring.

He must have believed me because he cupped my face and looked into my eyes, telling me sternly that this was my last chance. He told me that he believed I was sorry but, "This is it. Let me or my family down again and I'm gone. For good."

I was overjoyed. James and I were getting married and we would be the happy family I knew we could be.

Chapter 4

Our happiness was only damped by the fact we lived near to where I was raped. When I reported it to Victim Support, they suggested that I tried to move away from the area to avoid the bad memories and constant reminder. I'd put a request to the council and patiently waited.

James and I had been engaged for a few weeks when we received a letter to say that we'd been offered another home. While the flat was starting to feel cramped with the three of us living there, we were now being offered a two bedroomed house and we had three days to confirm whether we wanted it or not.

Of course, we went to have a look that evening, and couldn't believe how perfect it was for us. Although we could only look through the windows, we could see that it was lovely and smart. It was a new build so everything was pristine and it was crying out for a loving family to make it a home.

It wasn't just the house that was perfect either. It was opposite was a big square with a row of shops, and behind our street was a big field for us to take Luke to play in.

We accepted the offer the next day and moved into our beautiful new home shortly after.

We couldn't have been happier and we knew that the house was a perfect new start for us and our little family, which had now grown as we added two kittens, Susie and Jimmy.

Once we'd settled into Shepway, we began to make new friends. The neighbours were all really nice and welcoming. On one side was a lady called Christine. I remember that she had really long hair like Rapunzel that nearly reached her bottom. She was a nurse with two daughters who were both really pretty. They would often talk to me over the hedge and ask how Luke was; he just loved the attention!

On the other side was Barbara who had four cats. She loved her cats and would also look after any strays that needed help.

There was a huge house on the corner at the end of the road. It had a massive garden and the little boy there was always inviting Luke to play. His name was Archie and he was a little older than Luke, the two of them became such firm friends that if we were going out for the day we'd invite Archie along too.

As lovely as the neighbours were, and as nice as the house was, having the huge row of shops opposite our house soon became a massive problem. Older kids would hang around the shops and not only was it really intimidating to walk through, but they were so noisy at night that it started to affect Luke's sleep. He was tired and irritable all the time and could never seem to catch up on his sleep because as soon as we got him settled, the noise from over the road would start. As well as the kids and the various arguments that would go on, there were cars with loud music pulling up to drop off and pick up. We were fairly sure there was drug dealing going on too as the police were frequently there.

We knew we couldn't carry on like this so we put in for a mutual exchange. A mutual exchange is where the local council allows tenants to swap properties as long as they make the arrangements themselves. We were looking to swap for a similar sized house but in another area.

We knew that the exchange might take a while, so we made

the best of it whilst we were there and have some happy and memorable times.

I can remember Jenny and I coming home one day to a sea of people outside our house.

We'd just bought a new automatic car and James not being used to the controls, had driven straight into our porch instead of reversing out!

When I saw what had happened I froze. I was terrified that James was hurt, or worse. I started shaking and crying. Jenny ran towards the house telling me to stay back with Luke just in case.

Thankfully James was absolutely fine and having the porch there had saved any major damage to the house. The crowd subsided as fast as it had gathered and we reported the damage to the council, they sent someone out to us straight away to inspect the house and to make sure it was safe for us to stay in. Luckily it was; what a relief.

Once everyone had gone and James and I had both calmed down we even had a little giggle about it all – something like that could only happen to us!

Sadly, even though the house was fine and we could stay there, the car was completely trashed and beyond repair. James was miserable without his car. It was like his independence had been taken away from him and although it couldn't be helped we did wonder how we'd cope with public transport.

We were fortunate, just as they had been before and would be many times in the future, Jenny and Rich were there for us. A few nights later they sat us down and made an amazing offer. They were going to buy a new car and would be happy to give us their old one. We couldn't believe their generosity, and whatever happens I don't think we'll ever be able to truly thank them for everything they did for us then and have continued to do since.

Once we'd recovered from the shock of the accident, we started to make plans for our wedding. We were both so excited and set a date for 11 October, 2003. We talked about where we should get married and as I still suffered with nerves; I didn't think I could cope with the idea of walking down a big aisle. Churches always seemed huge and imposing and the idea of a ceremony that was massively religious really put me off.

Whenever I got drunk I would make a show of myself. I'd always try to make myself the centre of attention and would say or do things to make people notice me but oddly enough when I was sober, I was the complete opposite. I hated people seeing me or judging me, so the last thing I wanted to do on my wedding day was to give anyone the opportunity to do that.

James was happy to go along with what I wanted and together we decided that Maidstone Registry Office was the perfect location for us. It was small, intimate and meant I wouldn't feel too self-conscious. As it was by the river, we knew we'd be able to get lots of nice photographs too.

In the run up to our wedding, we were still drinking heavily every weekend. Occasionally we would smoke cannabis too. I loved the feeling that the cannabis gave me – making me all happy and giggly, so I couldn't see the harm in it. The only side effect I hated was how hungry it made me. In any one sitting I would eat chocolate bars, takeaways, popcorn, peanuts, crumpets, and cereal. Whatever there was in the cupboards I'd eat it and I wouldn't stop until there was nothing left.

Of course, this was really unhealthy and, not surprisingly, I started to put on weight. It was the first time in my life, including my pregnancy; that I'd ever gained weight and it started to really get me down – especially with my big day looming!

A few weeks before the wedding, I had a very rare drink with my dad. In my usual style I got really drunk and for some reason I ended up telling him about the cannabis. At the time he told me he was okay with it, and I went to bed happy and drunk. The next day though, he'd completely changed. He told me he was disgusted with me, and because of what I'd told him, he and my mum wouldn't be contributing to our wedding and neither of them would be coming.

I was devastated. We'd never been a tight family but we'd been a little closer since Luke was born. I really couldn't believe they wouldn't be there to give me away and to share our special day.

Once I'd recovered from the initial shock I decided on a plan. If anything, their news just made me more determined to have our big day as planned. At the time, my Nan was living in London and as soon as she found out what had happened she decided she would come to all of my dress fittings and do whatever she could to help with the planning. I was overwhelmed by her kindness and asked if she would consider giving me away. We'd always been close and I couldn't think of anything more perfect than having her walk me down the aisle. She told me she would be honoured, and that was that.

This wasn't the only time I can remember my Nan being there for me when I really needed her. When I was heavily pregnant with Luke and was still living with mum and dad they went on holiday. I stayed with her because I felt safer if something happened with the baby and sure enough I went into Labour two weeks before I was due. I was terrified and in agony with the labour pains, but Nan stayed with me the whole time and was there when Luke was born.

The wedding was a couple of months away when the news came through that our application for a mutual exchange had been successful. Our new home was a little smaller, but was in a much nicer area near Maidstone town centre. Best of all, it was closer to James' family, including his brother Josh who lived just around the corner.

The local school was also lovely and I managed to get Luke a place there. He was only four, so he was one of the youngest and I was a little worried about how he'd settle in, but Jenny was just starting work there as a dinner lady, and so I knew he would be looked after and have her to keep an eye on him. I needn't have worried at all as Luke settled in really quickly and made loads of new friends.

After a few months, I saw that another job was coming up as a dinner lady and I decided to apply for it myself. I got the job and was thrilled, I felt really proud of myself.

I was still drinking heavily and smoking regularly too, this meant that I was constantly late for work due to the terrible hangovers I was still suffering with. I don't know how, but I managed to get away with it. I would run into the dinner hall as fast as I could and hope nobody saw me, barely looking anyone in the eye in case they shouted at me. Looking back, it was really unfair to my workmates who were covering for me and I was putting Jenny in a horrible position as everyone knew we were related.

I honestly didn't stop and think more about how bad I was being to her and everyone else. Instead, I was just glad I'd managed to make it in at all as the hangovers were getting much worse and lasting much longer. I spent nearly every shift wishing it was over as I felt so ill.

With everything happening at once, the wedding soon crept up on us and it seemed that all of a sudden the big day was only weeks away! We both had our Hen and Stag nights booked and we were really looking forward to them.

I was going to a place called Victoria's which had a Robbie Williams tribute act on. Victoria's was a great night out, whatever the occasion; you paid forty pound for a meal and all inclusive drinks all night and I couldn't wait to get there. I was thrilled that my Nan and Jenny were coming too.

Sadly, Alison couldn't make it. I was devastated at the time and it still upsets me that she wasn't there, although I know I was to blame as I hadn't made enough effort to get her to come. After I met James, I wasn't a very good friend to Alison; she was there for me whenever I needed her but I can't say the same in return and I didn't deserve her.

As I knew it would be, my Hen night was very eventful! I didn't eat much of the meal but I made the most of the bar. By the time the Robbie act came on I was wrecked and couldn't leave the poor guy alone.

Because my future mother in law was there, it wasn't the best idea to be so forward but I was too drunk to either care or notice and at the end of the night Jenny caught me giving him my phone number. She quickly took it out of my hand and the next morning I was mortified.

I wanted to be completely honest with James though, especially as our wedding was our big second chance, and as soon as I woke up I told him all about Robbie and the phone number incident. He put it down to hen night antics and we've never spoken about it since.

I took Luke off to see Nan in London while James went out for his Stag do. He spent the day paintballing with his friends and an evening at a strip-club – tacky I know! Because of the problems I'd had with trusting him in the past I think he expected me to go mad when he told me their plans. I managed to put it to the back of my mind though as I just wanted him to be able to have a good time for once.

The next day I was a little sharp with him and I did grill him about what happened. He was completely honest with me: his friends had paid for a few lap-dances and he seemed a little worried about telling me. I could tell from the way that he was talking that the dances had meant nothing to him and that his night out had been more about seeing his friends than some strippers so for once I didn't bite.

Before we knew it, it was the day before our wedding. My Nan had come down early so that we could spend the day together, we had lots of fun getting our nails done and going to lunch. Nan was staying with me that night as James was staying with his parents. We all met in the pub in the afternoon to say goodbye and have a few drinks together.

Once we arrived home, Nan and I had a few drinks and Jenny popped in. Sam, James sister-in-law, had also come round and as it got later, I started to get more and more nervous – I really don't know how I slept that night!

The next morning the house was noisy and busy. My cousin Kym came over with her daughter Faith. Faith was my little flower girl with Luke being our page boy. I was so nervous I couldn't stand it and I went out to buy some vodka to calm my nerves. Kym and I had a quick drink while I tried to relax then we walked to the hairdressers to get my hair and make-up done.

The salon was just a few minutes' walk away and was owned by a local character called Philippe. He was well known for being loud, funny and a transvestite. He was petite, with permed hair and always wore a skirt with his top. Philippe always looked amazing.

He was bubbly and infectiously happy which I really needed that morning. Best of all, he let us smoke in the salon so I was able to calm down as he worked on my hair.

I hadn't had a hair trial. Philippe didn't believe in them. He said his work was always perfect and I just had to have faith in him. I did and had chosen a simple, elegant style with my hair tied up and some curls at the front. He said that they would soften my face and make me look like a princess so we went with that, and sure enough it looked perfect. I hugged him to say thank you and hurried to put my dress on.

I'd no sooner got dressed than it was time to leave. Jenny and Rich came to pick Nan and I up to take us to the Registry Office. Jenny had decorated the car with flowers and bows and our photographer took a few pictures of us standing by it. Then it was time to go and I very excitedly climbed in.

We had to drive through the centre of town to reach the Registry Office and I started to feel really self-conscious. For some reason, I felt overdressed to be driving through somewhere I went most days and I was very nervous.

I remember feeling like this a few times throughout the day. Now, those feelings seem like such a waste. I would love for James and myself to renew our vows one day. I know that I would enjoy the day more and cherish the memories.

On the day though, I just swallowed the feelings back and tried to make the most of our special day.

We had chosen the Toploader song "Dancing in the Moonlight" to walk down the aisle too. It was a song James and I loved and we both decided that we wanted something a little different. As the song struck up, Luke walked down the aisle first holding a pillow with our rings on it. We'd dressed him in a suit that he'd helped to choose and he looked amazing, beaming all the way down the aisle until he reached James and handed the ring cushion over. After that Faith walked down the aisle looking like a little princess, and then finally Nan and myself.

Knowing that I would be so nervous, James and I had chosen the quickest service and shortest set of vows we could possibly choose. We both felt a little self-conscious but as soon as I reached James and felt his hand grasp mine, everything felt right.

I actually found that I enjoyed saying my vows and as the Registrar pronounced us as: "husband and wife" I felt completely calm and peaceful.

Once we'd signed the register we walked back up the aisle and outside the Office to have our photographs taken and to greet our guests. It was a gorgeous hot day, all of the family children were running up and down in the gardens and by the river. It was the perfect family day.

After our photographs, we set off with James' family and my Nan for a lovely meal. Our reception was held at The Orchard Spot in Downswood, we had an amazing day. I hadn't set out to drink too much but of course I did and as a result I don't remember too much of the reception. What I do remember though is getting really upset when it was over and we had to leave: I couldn't believe that the day we'd spent so long planning was over and I cried my eyes out as I said goodbye to everyone.

Josh and Sam arranged for us to stay in a really posh hotel for our wedding present at The Tudor Park for our wedding night. Because I'd had so much to drink I can't honestly remember what the hotel looked like properly but I knew I'd never been in a place that high-class before. We arrived at reception which was easily the biggest room I've ever been in and they had a butler take us up to our room. Inside was a gigantic bed and on a little table nearby was a chilled bottle of champagne and some chocolates. By that time, all I wanted to do was relax, so I took off my dress, took the pins out of my hair and scrubbed my make up off. As much as I'd felt fantastic in them, I felt overdressed and silly sitting in a hotel room in them. James and I drank the champagne and excitedly talked through the day.

We were so full of adrenaline that neither of us could sleep, so we sat up opening our cards. They were all full of money people had given us for our honeymoon. As I opened the cards, James was writing a list of who'd given us what so we could thank them later.

We'd never expected anything and were completely surprised by everyone's generosity. We were already looking forward to our honeymoon, but the money meant that we could enjoy it all the more.

Once we'd finished opening all the cards, we put the money out onto the bed and then stared at it all. We were so overwhelmed and happy that we started jumping up and down, screaming and giggling. Before I knew it we were jumping down on the money covered bed. The people in the room next to us must have thought there was something very strange going on but we were completely lost in the moment – grateful that we had each other and all of these people who loved us.

Our honeymoon was to Rhodes in Greece and was another present. This time it was from my Nan. She had got together with Rich and Jenny and decided that we needed a break, so while she paid for the trip, they were going to look after Luke.

It was an all-inclusive holiday so we knew that we were going to have a great time without the worry of having to pay for anything other than souvenirs while we were there.

The day we left, Luke was poorly, he suffered with Croup quite regularly and just as we were getting ready to go, he started to come down with a bout of it. Of course, it made leaving him very difficult but Jenny convinced us that they'd be fine and Luke was happy to stay with them so we set off!

From the second we arrived there, we made full use of the all-inclusive bar, and as you can imagine we missed a lot of the holiday, either being hung over or ill in bed.

We also argued a lot about the way that the drink changed me as a person. I was really nasty to James on a few occasions and he left me in the bar alone twice, storming out because of the way I was behaving towards him. Not only was I making a show of myself but I was trying to make him look stupid.

I woke up a few times with a terrible hangover. James and I weren't speaking because of my behaviour and it didn't help that although I was saying sorry, I didn't know what I was apologising for as I couldn't remember what I'd said or done.

The problem was that because the drink was free and on tap, I wanted to make the most of it and enjoy the freedom of not having Luke or any other responsibilities with me.

One of the memories which really sticks with me, for good and bad, is on our last day. As with many resorts, we had to check out in the morning but our flights weren't scheduled to leave until early evening.

The friends we had made were in the same situation, so we all met up by the bar – where we all got completely hammered! We figured that it was the last few hours of our holiday and we wanted to make the most of them. So we got drunker and drunker – at one point I was behind the bar, in a silly hat serving out the drinks!

We had arranged for Luke to stay with Jenny and Rich until the next day so we thought that one last session wouldn't hurt anyone, and we had a brilliant time with all of the new friends we'd made.

Once the bus came to pick us up, the party was over and on the hour long journey to the airport I started to sober up. Once we arrived at the airport, my hangover was kicking in! It wasn't until we got to the check-in that we realised I'd left my passport at the hotel, behind the bar, of all places! That in itself was bad enough but we'd also used up all of our money and the taxi back to the hotel to get my passport would cost fifty pounds.

We had no choice but to go back and get it but we didn't know how, until one of the couples we'd made friends with offered to help us out.

Although all was saved, in the four hours since checking out of the hotel and the bar to catching our flight, my hangover had arrived and was horrendous and the flight back was awful for me. I felt sick and my head was pounding. Normally, I just started to drink again but this time my body wouldn't let me and although James and I ordered vodka each on the plane, I didn't drink any of mine. It was a very long journey!

We spoke to Luke everyday and knew he was still poorly. He was in good hands with Jenny and Rich. Now on our way home, I was desperate to see my little boy.

Chapter 5

Once we got back from our honeymoon we started to settle into family life. Because we'd moved house, I had to leave my job in the school kitchen, and James and I decided I should apply for a job in the play school next to Luke's school. I got the job and started straight away.

I worked at the play school for about a year and made some new friends including Wendy, who lived opposite us with her partner and two children. Her son Riley was a few years above Luke in school but Wendy and I got chatting and soon became friends. She worked part time in our local shop so I saw her quite often.

We'd settled in really well into our new home and things were just calming down when James and I got the wonderful news that we were going to have a new arrival!

I was overjoyed to be pregnant again. I'd wanted another baby for years and couldn't wait to start getting things ready for our new baby. Unlike when I was pregnant with Luke, I worked all the way through this pregnancy, still enjoying the job but finding it very difficult. I remember being tired all the time. The pregnancy itself was completely different. I was really sick early on and then continued to bleed throughout. We were heavily monitored and always seemed to be at one appointment or another. I was also really emotional. Anything and everything would set me off in floods of tears. I remember watching the programme "One Born Every Minute" and being near-on hysterical.

Of course, James hadn't known me while I was pregnant with Luke, so I could only tell him how different the two experiences were.

As well as being sick, tired and emotional, I found that I really missed having a drink. Stopping drinking had been easy enough as I loved the baby completely and there was no way I would do anything that might put him or her in danger, but that didn't stop me wanting one – or resenting anyone else for being able to drink.

Looking back its funny how quickly I stopped drinking because of the health risks to my baby, yet I never stopped and really thought about the risks to my own health.

During the week, work and Luke would keep me busy and so I wouldn't think about what I was missing out on, but at the weekends things were different. I remember this particular summer being one where we had lots of wedding invitations. Hardly a month went by without an invitation and I ended up refusing to go to most of them. James went alone and made up an excuse as to why I wasn't there. We never talked about what was happening, so I was able to lie to him and myself and say that I felt unwell or over-tired because of the pregnancy. He'd pass that message on and nobody was any the wiser.

The truth was that I hated seeing anyone being able to do what I couldn't and because James had been my drinking partner, I hated seeing him enjoy himself most of all, when I felt I couldn't have fun without a drink.

He's never been a big drinker so normal weekday evenings wouldn't bother me at all, but as soon as the weekend hit he would want to have a few drinks with his mates: at a wedding, or as we watched TV and I would seethe. I felt as though he was taunting me every time he had a drink so I refused to put myself in a position where he had the chance.

He wasn't doing it deliberately, I'm not even sure if he realised what was going through my mind.

In addition, I was vile to him when he came home. I caused countless arguments and would ignore him for days on end for daring to leave me alone.

It's only looking back on these times that I realise I'd gone from being a weekend drinker or a social drinker to someone with a problem. I certainly couldn't see or accept that at the time. It would take a long time before I could start to look at myself as a person with a problem and, for now, I was stuck putting my fingers in my ears and pretending not to hear anyone who tried to discuss things with me.

As the pregnancy went on, my moods got worse and I would start a fight about almost anything. The arguments were always with James and they were loud and sometimes violent. I don't know, to this day, whether I was so argumentative because of the hormones, or because I wasn't coping without having a drink, but my moods were awful and I lashed out at James all the time.

At the end of a very long, tiring and stressful pregnancy, our beautiful boy Liam was born in September 2004, weighing 6lbs 6 oz. Given how bad a pregnancy I'd had, my labour was surprisingly "normal." James was a brilliant birthing partner – even if I did bruise his hand from squeezing it. Jenny and Rich brought Luke to the hospital to meet his baby brother. Luke was over the moon and to see them bonding was brilliant. I stayed in hospital that night with Liam. I just wanted to have him to myself for just one night before we went home and settled into a routine. The following day we went home and became a family of four. I'd decided through my pregnancy that I wanted to try breastfeeding but I only lasted a few days because it really wasn't for me.

It's no exaggeration to say that the next few years were hard!

Liam was a very unsettled baby, and up until he was three he didn't sleep for more than a few hours at a time. We tried everything to get him to sleep and even the Health Visitors were baffled by why he wasn't sleeping.

Deep down, I always felt that the reason Liam was so unsettled was because of all the arguing we did while I was carrying him. I was sure, and still am to an extent, that it had to have had an effect on him.

I think this was my turning point back to the drink. I was so stressed, trying to cope as new mum again and I felt like I needed a drink to help me and I was drinking all the time, in fact, I drank every night.

Liam never seemed to sleep. He'd be awake throughout the night with us having about three hours sleep at most, and so I'd start everyday exhausted and drained. Parenting manuals, Health Visitors and well-meaning friends would always say that I should catch up on sleep while he was sleeping.

They'd tell me that things like housework could wait and I should just lie down with him. I could see the sense in it but he never slept for any more than twenty minutes at a time during the day, so I never got the opportunity. I was permanently tired and struggling to cope.

James was working full time so for the majority of the day it was me and Liam while Luke was at school. As the day would wear on, Liam would become more and more agitated because he was overtired and was probably picking up on how stressed out I was. By the time James came home, at six in the evening, I was ready to cry.

I remember being tired all the time and feeling that I had nobody to help me. James was working hard to provide for us, but I missed him and by the time he came in I was too tired to talk to him properly and he was tired from his day at work, so our relationship started to suffer. Jenny and Rich were also working, so although they would call in to check on us and help out whenever they could, I was, for the most part, on my own.

As well as feeling tired and stressed, I quickly found out that having a baby who wasn't "easy" was a very lonely experience. Like many new mothers, I didn't want to stay in the house all day, and it was a lot harder to stay awake and functioning if I had nothing to do and nowhere to go. Luckily Josh's wife Sam had had twins just a few months before and we would get together and go to baby groups. The problem for me was that unlike Liam, their twins Phoebe and Noel were excellent sleepers and it seemed that all of the mothers in the groups had "perfect" babies too. I felt alone, like I was doing something wrong. I loved Liam with all my heart, but I was beginning to feel like a failure and I felt like there was a big divide between me and the other mothers for how easy they seemed to have it and how hard things were for me.

As bad as I felt, I never resented Sam. She was a brilliant mother and always seemed so organised and happy with the twins. If anything I felt like a failure when I compared myself to her. She never made me feel like that though. She just listened when I needed to let off steam and was always on hand with a hug and some helpful advice. Before we had children the same age, I hadn't really known her as a person in her own right; she was always Josh's wife. Having Liam and the twins being so close in age meant that as they played together I could really get to know Sam and she became a really good friend to me.

It wasn't long before I started to rely on a drink in the evenings to calm me down. James would come home and I'd pour myself a long drink. The first would always be the strongest and although I didn't use a measure, I knew I was putting at least a triple shot of vodka in the glass before topping it up.

That first drink of the evening was my escape from the day. As soon as I started drinking, I could feel the tension and stress leaving me. Finally, I was happy and relaxed and could think clearly, or so I thought!

For a while, that was our routine, and I honestly don't know how I managed it. I just carried on without sleep; going through the motions of taking Luke to school, spending the day looking after Liam, and being a housewife. I was exhausted, but that drink at the end of the day made it seem easier.

One night, I called into the shop to see Wendy. It had been a while since I was able to have a chat and see how she was. The man she was serving was putting a bottle of alcohol on "the tick" and I wondered what was going on. Wendy explained that Fred, the shop owner, let customers put the things they couldn't afford onto a tab and then pay at the end of the week. I'd never heard of that before but she explained I could put alcohol, cigarettes and anything else I wanted on the tab. I quickly started to think that it could help us out.

Much to James' disgust, I started to put half a bottle of vodka a night on my tab. Half a bottle cost five pound, so over the course of the week nights alone our tab was mounting up. Quite often, the half bottle wouldn't be enough and I'd need to go to the shop again midway through the evening for another bottle. I'd always have an excuse ready in my head just in case I needed it. Most of the time I'd blame a bad day with Liam, or I'd pick a fight with James and accuse him of drinking more than his fair share. It caused no end of rows but if James ever said no, or tried to put his foot down, I would sulk or cause an argument. I told him that I needed the drink because I was so tired. In the end, he had to just accept it.

Because I was drinking so much, I began to change again, slipping back into my old habits. There were many mornings when I would find James on the sofa. He explained that it was because my behaviour was so erratic but I wouldn't be able to remember what I'd done or said the night before. I also started to suffer with hangovers again. I'd feel sick all day.

I had many mornings where I couldn't even remember going to bed the night before. James fell into a routine of tidying up after me. He'd never let the children come down to a mess so if I passed out, he would always make sure I got to bed and that the front room was tidied.

I started to be able to tell within ten minutes of waking up whether the hangover was going to be a good or a bad one. There were even times when I'd feel so ill that I'd wake up in the middle of the night with the start of a bad come-down and when a bad one hit, I'd find it really hard to function.

My hangovers always gave me a pounding head and sickness. Some days I would spend the whole day throwing up but it would never make me feel better. It never put me off my drink though, I hear people say "I'm never drinking again" when they have a hangover, for me this was just part of my life.

Getting out of bed initially was the hardest and I'd hit the snooze button on the alarm far too many times, meaning that we'd be late for the school run. Even after I'd managed to get us all up and out, if I was feeling particularly rough I couldn't function properly around other people so I'd simply make up an excuse about having a bad night with Liam so I wouldn't have to face anyone. After that, I'd go home stocked up with Red Bull and junk food and laze on the sofa with Liam sitting playing and watching the TV.

The one thing that remained constant however bad or mild my hangover was that I would still have a drink the following night. If it had been a good day hangover wise, I'd hit the vodka hard that night, but a bad day would mean I'd have just enough drink to take the edge off my stress. I'd call it the difference between "power drinking" and "feeling the need."

During the week, I'd try to limit myself to a half bottle of vodka, but at the weekends I'd let myself go and enjoy the drinking a little more. I'd allow myself a full litre each night, sometimes more, and wouldn't stop until I passed out.

It was those Saturday and Sunday mornings where my hangovers would be the worst and they meant that we couldn't do anything together as a family. It never put me off though, and many days the only thing that would keep me going would be looking forward to the evening when I could start drinking again.

Liam was about eighteen months old when I decided to go back to work. I'd loved working at the nursery with a great team and the lovely kids; I really missed it while I was off looking after Liam and Luke. I was hoping that having the job and the routine would make me feel a little more positive again.

So I approached them and asked if I could come back and was thrilled when they said they'd love to have me back.

What hit me at first was how hard it was to get us all up and ready in the morning. Before, it didn't matter how I looked or if Liam was washed and dressed as long as we got Luke to school on time but now I had to look presentable and Liam had to be ready for the day as well. We soon fell into a routine and I discovered a few short cuts such as pulling my hair into a ponytail rather than straightening it all. That made us a lot faster in the morning, and meant that if I had an extra snooze it didn't matter as much.

There were days where we were a little more chaotic than others, and some days I'd have to stop off at the shop to buy Luke some sandwiches as I'd forgotten or hadn't had time to get his packed lunch ready.

My manager Marie said that I could bring Liam into work with me. She was happy for him to be there for a few mornings to help out with childcare but only on the understanding that I was there to work and Liam couldn't take all of my time or attention. Luckily, he loved it there and settled in really well. He'd play with the other children and was really independent so it didn't seem to bother him that I was helping or holding other children.

The days there must have been tiring him out too as he started to sleep for longer at night and settled into a better routine. Things were working out perfectly.

Because I enjoyed the job so much, I tried to be a little more controlled with the amount I drank. I would make sure I ate a proper meal in the evening before I started drinking and because of that, I wouldn't suffer quite as much the next day. There were still days when I was too ill to go into work but on those days I'd feel so angry with myself for letting the other girls down, and so bored at home, that it taught me a lesson and I'd make sure I was more careful the next time.

James and I were still arguing quite a lot, especially on nights where I'd had too much to drink and at the weekends where I didn't have work to keep me sober.

Liam was two when I found out I was pregnant again. I told James and it's safe to say that the news was as much of a surprise for him as it was for me.

We had a lot of thinking to do about how we'd make it work financially and practically, things were already a little tight.

Our house only had two bedrooms and we'd only just got settled from our last major change. Liam's sleeplessness had unsettled all of us and the timing of this pregnancy wasn't great. As well as that, we were concerned that because I'd been so ill during my pregnancy with Liam I'd be the same with this one and would have to give up my job. That would put a huge strain on us both but especially on James as the only person bringing any money into the house.

Still, we were determined to make things work and I decided that for as long as I could, I'd carry on working with Marie's support.

Beyond that, we would just have to hope that this little bundle might enjoy sleeping a little more than their big brother had. As much as we loved Liam, he had been such hard work that we hoped for an easier time.

Chapter 6

Even though we'd been through a lot with Liam, I was really looking forward to having another baby. I loved working with children and, although I wouldn't admit it, I was secretly hoping to have a girl this time, to complete our family.

James was initially shocked and apprehensive, but once he was used to the idea we started to get excited together. Liam had started to sleep a little better so the prospect of having another new born baby didn't seem quite as horrifying.

I found pregnancy so much easier this time round and in general I felt happier. My moods seemed less erratic, and so James and I argued less. I suppose at the time I should have realised that James and I got on better when I wasn't drinking, but it would take a lot longer for that message to get through to me.

We were so excited by the time I got to four months, that neither of us could wait any longer and we paid for a private scan to tell us whether we were having a boy or a girl. We took Luke with us as we wanted him to feel included and we were ecstatic when they told us we were expecting a baby girl!

I had a lovely pregnancy and in late August 2007 I woke up to find that my waters had broken. I hadn't had this happen with either Luke or Liam and so we rushed up to the hospital. They examined me when we arrived and discovered meconium in the waters. They told me that this meant my baby had pooed inside me. Because I was in labour and had lost some of the waters, they needed to act quickly because if a baby swallows the meconium it can be very dangerous for them.

They put me on a drip to speed up the labour and explained that if things didn't progress as quickly as they expected then I might need to have a C-section. Luckily though I had a quick labour and they didn't need to get involved, and my beautiful girl Ami was born naturally weighing 6lb 1oz.

Jenny and Rich brought Luke and Liam up to the hospital to us. It was so emotional seeing them both happy and proud to meet their new baby sister. Because I'd had a few complications in my labour, the hospital insisted that I stayed in overnight, so James went home with the boys and I stayed with Ami.

The doctors and midwives kept a careful eye on us and we didn't seem to get a moment to ourselves. Ami had to be carefully monitored to make sure there were no complications. Although I should have felt anxious, she seemed to be absolutely fine and was sailing through all of her observations. She was alert and feeding well so they seemed happy enough and I was just thrilled to have my daughter to myself for the night. I'd decided to give breastfeeding another go and this time I fed her for a few weeks.

When we left the hospital, I found that Ami was a brilliant baby; she was easily settled and slept much better for longer. As I've already mentioned, I'd felt for a long time that the reason Liam was so unsettled was because I'd had a difficult and stressful pregnancy. As things had been so much easier while I was pregnant with Ami, and I was so much calmer throughout, it was now blindingly obvious to me that the pregnancies had made a difference.

Of course, while I was grateful that Ami was placid and slept well, I felt so guilty that Liam hadn't and I was to blame. I couldn't see it at the time but all of the negativity I was letting out and the tension I was causing had affected all of my relationships; it was just that it was the most obvious with Liam.

As I look at Liam now, he's a happy and confident little boy with a heart of gold and tons of friends and it proves to me that security plays a huge part in a child's happiness. I've learned a lot of lessons in the past few years while in sobriety but this is one of the biggest.

Ami and I had been home for a few weeks and something strange happened. For as long as I can remember, I'd have a "funny" sensation where I lose my concentration and "zone out" for a few seconds. I'd be fine after and so I never thought much of it. One night though, I was in the kitchen making Ami's bottle and it happened again. The next thing I knew, I was lying on the sofa with everyone looking at me.

James managed to calmly explain that I'd had a fit and that there was an ambulance on the way. He'd also phoned Jenny and Rich to get them to come over urgently to look after the children and off we went.

I didn't know what had happened and was terrified. The only thing I noticed was that my mouth felt very sore from where I'd gritted my teeth and bitten down hard during my seizure.

When we got to the hospital they told me I'd need to stay in overnight and would have to have a CT scan. I hated the tube machine I had to lie in while they took the images, it made me feel claustrophobic. I decided there and then that I never wanted another one.

The following day, the doctor came round; having looked at the results of the scan and explained that they thought it was just a one off fit. They told me to come back if I had another but didn't seem too concerned and I was allowed to go home.

Although the fit had really scared me, I tried to put it to the back of my mind and carry on as normal. I started drinking again and soon got the taste for it. Just as I had before, I started to behave wildly and erratically, and poor James suffered the most.

When I drank I was out of control. It was like I needed to test the relationship with James, or see how far I could push him. I'd done the same when I was at home with my parents, all in a bid to get attention. It wasn't until years later, when I was sober, that I stopped being so destructive. I could finally see, without the drink, that these relationships were valid on their own and didn't need to be tested or tried. Whether they're with friends, family, my husband or my children, I can see the true value of the relationships in my life.

Back then, as well as testing him I gave James plenty of reasons to doubt me and our relationship. One of the worst things I did to James was to flirt with other men in front of him. Sometimes, I'd throw myself at his friends, which is something I'm desperately ashamed of now, and could never contemplate doing sober.

Almost everything I did when drunk was done with the aim of drawing attention to myself and between having a fiery nature, a horrible temper and the paranoia that came with heavy drinking, I would always find the wrong type of attention.

As well as my drinking, we had to cope with moving again. Although we loved our home and the area, the house was just too small, with only two bedrooms we had all three of the children squashed into one room.

Just as we had before, we put our home on a home swapping website and we got lots of offers. We'd already decided that we wanted to keep Luke and Liam at the same schools so we needed something which was near to where we were.

We found a three bedroom house in an area a little further than we wanted, which was also quite a rough area. The house was so lovely and big though that we were sold. We just decided to go for it and vowed that we'd keep ourselves to ourselves if there was any trouble.

We didn't have to wait long for trouble though. We were unpacking our moving van when the house opposite us was raided. Literally, we were just pulling up in the van when a police car with sirens screamed to a halt and two police officers started hammering on the door. True to our promise, we kept our heads down and started to get settled.

Although I had to catch a bus to take Luke and Liam to school, we soon settled into a routine.

My Nan came to stay with us a few days later. Her original reason was to see the new house and help us to settle in but when she arrived from London she had a surprise for us. Because it was our wedding anniversary coming up, she'd arranged for us to stay in a hotel for the night while she would look after the children. We were so excited and couldn't wait for a little time together.

I had a few drinks before we went and headed upstairs to get ready, but things didn't go to plan and when I came round from another fit; it looked like we wouldn't be getting our hotel break after all.

James took me to hospital straight away while Nan looked after the children.

Because I'd had a fit, the hospital didn't keep us waiting and I was seen by a doctor immediately. Thank goodness because I had another fit in front of him. When I came to I was on a hospital bed with James standing next to me – I had no recollection of getting there.

The doctor explained to us both that because I'd had a further two fits, they couldn't simply treat them as a "one off" anymore and that I would have to have some more tests including another brain scan.

The first scan had terrified me so much that I really didn't want another one and I certainly didn't want to go into that tunnel again but I knew I had to.

They did the scan and then referred me to Kings College Hospital in London for the results. These would take a few weeks, and I would have to wait for an appointment to be sent to me. Little did I know that those few weeks were going to be as awful for us as anything that had come before.

Chapter 7

After the disappointment of losing out on our hotel break, and the worry of the looming results, it was very difficult to focus, but James and I tried to carry on as normal and luckily we had plenty to look forward to.

Radio 1 had just announced that they were coming to Maidstone as part of their "Big Weekend." There were some brilliant musical acts on, as well as the main DJ's, and everyone wanted tickets. The Big Weekend would take place over a Saturday and Sunday night and was one of the biggest concerts we'd ever seen locally.

Unlike James, I wasn't really excited by the live music. It was the prospect of a whole day of drinking that I could look forward to. I had it planned in my head that I could sneak a bottle of vodka in with me and find a place away from the main stages where I could drink and have a laugh. Even though the music that James' band played wasn't really to my taste I'd always had a great time at his gigs, the atmosphere in the crowd was great, so the prospect of a huge gig where it would be even better was thrilling.

In the run up to the gig, Radio 1 had announced that the tickets would be given away randomly. Then they confirmed that the tickets would be handed out depending on postcodes and finally, they announced the addresses which had been chosen to receive tickets. Ours wasn't one of them and we were gutted; albeit for different reasons.

Within hours though, people who didn't want their tickets were selling them online, some of them were being sold for over a hundred pound each. There was no way we could afford to go and we were even more upset!

We decided we wouldn't let it get to us and so, on the first night we sat outside in the garden listening to the music. We could hear quite clearly, so at least we didn't miss the whole thing. However hearing it but not being able to see anything or be directly in the crowd, I felt we were missing out on the atmosphere and it made me want to go even more!

I bought a big bottle of vodka for the evening, and although we'd sat out drinking and enjoying what we could of the festival, I hadn't finished my share. So, I decided to save the rest for the next night. If I was in the mood, I could finish an entire bottle of vodka in one sitting. I'd make it so strong that if I was a little tired when I started drinking it would simply make me even more tired, so rather than getting drunk I'd just crash out. This night, I was out of sorts anyway and just didn't feel that I wanted to carry on drinking because it just reminded me of what we were missing out on.

The following day, Luke had his football practice. He played for a local team and they had a match every Sunday. James would go and watch him while I stayed at home with Liam and Ami, usually nursing a hangover. They hadn't been gone very long when James rang.

His brother Josh had been given two tickets for the Big Weekend by a friend. Sam wasn't bothered about going so Josh wondered if James wanted to go instead. He didn't really wait for an answer but said he'd be home in a while.

I was absolutely livid and by the time he got home from football with Luke, I'd worked myself into a foul mood. I was so jealous and wanted to go so badly that I couldn't believe James would go without me.

I was still angry when Josh came to pick James up and was even frosty with him too. They must have got the message as they quickly left.

I was stewing at home, thinking how unfair it was that they got to go and not me, when Sam called. There was a family barbeque on and invited me to go and spend the day with them. James had told me before he left to expect her calls but I didn't want to go out to a family do – I wanted to be out with James at the festival. I ignored all of her calls and she must have figured out that I was ignoring her because eventually she stopped.

Looking back, I can't believe how I reacted. At the time, I felt like I was acting so rationally. James was abandoning me and it felt like the worst betrayal in the world. Now, I can see I was acting like a spoiled child, but hindsight, as they say, is always perfect vision.

The betrayal felt all the worse because nobody was offering me a ticket, so as well as feeling jealous that James was getting to go, I was sore about the fact that nobody was thinking about me. It makes perfect sense that they wouldn't as, again when looking back, I can see that I was mean, selfish and horrible as a drunk. I was rude to anyone I took against, would cry for hours at a time and was often sick. I used to mix drinks to get as drunk as possible as fast as possible and because of that, my body couldn't take what I was pouring into it. I'd often, without any warning, just throw up in public. I felt terribly hard done by at the time, but why would anyone want to take me to a gig where I was going to drink all day and behave the way I did?

Although a lot had happened, it was still only morning and when I first saw the half-drunk bottle of vodka from the night before, I tried to ignore it. I didn't normally drink that early and besides I had three children to look after for the rest of the day. But I felt so hurt by James and abandoned by everyone else we knew that I started to crave a way to feel better. If I could just find something to get me through the rest of the day then it wouldn't be as much of a loss. So I poured myself a drink and was sure it would make me feel better.

It went down so well that before I knew it, I'd finished what was left in the bottle and by that point I'd got a taste for it. I just wanted more; I convinced myself that if James was allowed to party then so was I. The off licence was just over the road so I went and bought another bottle.

I carried on drinking, and it carried on going down just as nicely as the first bottle had. As I got drunker and drunker, I got angrier and angrier with James and I started trying to get in touch with him.

I sent a series of nasty text messages, telling him that I hated him for going without me and that I'd managed to get a ticket and that I was coming down to find him. Next, and I'll never know what possessed me to do this but I sent a message saying that Ami was ill and I was taking her to the hospital.

Rightly so, James was angry. He was having a good time with his brother and friends, who he rarely saw and I had gone too far. He told me later that he'd showed Josh the messages and Josh was angry too. At the time, the relationship between myself and Josh was already fractured. He and James had been really close before James and I got together but our time with the children, and his time with his, meant that they didn't see as much of each other. When they did it would inevitably end with me flying into a rage. It was very rare in those days that James would even ask if he could go out alone. The thought of a grown man having to ask his wife's permission to go out with his brother must sound horrifying, but I got so angry so quickly and was so jealous that James did anything for a quiet life; including lying to his family. They must have been able to see what was going on but James was loyal to me and the children and never told them how controlling or vicious I could be.

When I look back to how I acted when I was drinking, it was like I had an alter-ego. Drunk Emma and sober Emma were like my yin and yang. While sober Emma was quiet and shy, she was much nicer than drunk, vicious Emma but I couldn't see that. Sober Emma had no confidence, she blushed when she talked and was no fun at all. I could only see the part I wanted to blot out and it was the shy, unassuming part of me that I wanted to be gone.

As well as showing my messages to Josh, and I assume to the friends they were with; James had also contacted his parents to tell them he was concerned about me being drunk with the children. They came straight round and they too were furious with me.

By the time they arrived, I'd drunk a whole litre of vodka and I can't remember too much more of the day. I can recall Jenny telling me that I should be ashamed of myself and that I'd regret what I'd done in the morning. Rich hardly looked at me as they got the children ready to take them and by the time Luke, Liam and Ami were sitting ready to go at the bottom of the stairs, I could barely stand.

The next thing I remember was a loud banging at the door. It was Josh. He'd had enough by this point and although he'd told James to stay with their group of friends and not to worry as his mum and dad were coming to help, he had come to have it out with me. He hadn't told James and had instead said he was going early because of work the following day. But he was furious and started shouting at me. Nothing I was saying was making sense as I was so drunk and the children were starting to get really upset by the shouting, Jenny and Rich tried desperately to calm us both down.

Rich and Jenny must have been able to tell that Josh was

about to really lose his temper and they intervened. They told him to go home and saw him off then told me they were taking the children.

They left, and I was alone. With the children gone, there was nothing for me to do but stagger to bed. When I came to, it was about four am and I had the stirrings of a hangover. I felt sick and dehydrated. I could cope with the physical symptoms of what had happened but I knew that there had been trouble too, although I couldn't remember it at the time. I just lay with my head in my hands, wondering how I'd get myself out of this mess, whatever that might be, thinking "oh shit."

James woke me coming in and as he came into the bedroom he could barely bring himself to look at me. He told me that he couldn't believe what I'd done. He said flatly that our marriage was over and that he'd be leaving me in the morning. Then he climbed into bed, turned away from me and that was that.

I remember feeling utterly hysterical. I could hardly remember anything – how could he leave me for doing things I couldn't remember? I felt sure that he didn't mean it and that he was just trying to make me feel worse.

I tried to go back to sleep but tossed and turned for a while before deciding to go down to the kitchen to get a drink of water. I knocked it back and went to walk back upstairs, feeling sick and shaken. Walking up the stairs was like walking around on a ship in stormy seas. It felt like the floor was moving and I couldn't get my balance.

I didn't know if I'd dreamed the conversation with James, but when I went back into the bedroom and saw him lying there, I felt sure that I must have dreamt it all. He wouldn't be asleep in our bed if he was leaving me. So I climbed in beside him and put my arm around him. Within seconds, he'd shaken me roughly away and told me to get off him. Then the reality hit me, it was real. I knew there was an argument to come in the morning.

I tried to roll over to get back to sleep but couldn't. I felt so ill, and knowing that James was so angry with me there was no way I could relax. I lay in the darkness waiting for James' alarm to go off as he had work that Monday morning. I decided that if I made him and myself a cup of coffee before he went to work then we could quickly sort things out and everything would be fine.

As I was lying there, the memories of the night before started to become clearer. I remembered Jenny and Rich collecting the children and being disgusted with me. I remembered Josh shouting furiously at me. And I remembered what I'd done to James to punish him for leaving me alone.

None of it seemed real but I felt sick to my stomach as I pieced it all together.

When James' alarm went off, he climbed out of bed without even looking at me and went straight into the bathroom. I got up and, as I'd planned, went straight down to the kitchen, feeling more and more ill with every passing second.

The next thing I heard was the doorbell ringing. It was a guy James worked with and he answered the door to him. I normally went out to say hello but this time I didn't dare. I overheard James saying he'd be a few minutes as he had to sort out a situation and telling his workmate what a nutcase he had for a wife.

Then he came into the kitchen. He handed me his wedding ring and told me he'd be back to collect the rest of his things later on.

I wasn't sure what was happening because he'd been so calm earlier. I'd felt so certain that he was joking or making an idle threat. I had nothing to say but as he handed me the ring I tried to hold his hand. He pulled away roughly and I started pleading,

"I'm so sorry. I really don't know what happened. I can't remember. I had too much to drink. Come on babe, you know I didn't mean it."

I knew then how much I loved James and how I couldn't survive without him. I might have had a funny way of showing it but I really did adore him and I simply didn't work without us being together.

I don't blame him for wanting to leave, I didn't deserve him and my possessiveness was strangling him. He deserved so much better than me and the way I treated him, which wasn't much better than bullying.

Normally, he responded to my pleading and let me have my own way or backed down but I'd never seen him like this. The way he looked at me was cold and determined. I thought I knew his face inside out but when he looked so disgusted with me, I suddenly felt very small and scared.

This time he wouldn't back down. This time, he stood and faced me and snapped

"I will be back later on for my things Emma. I will not be coming home and nothing you can say will change my mind. I've had ENOUGH; you make sure you have my things ready for me."

With that, he left me to dissolve into tears.

Once he'd gone I sat and tried to work through what had happened more clearly. All I wanted to do was cry but it was a Monday and I needed to see to the children. Rich phoned that morning to say that although he and Jenny had taken Luke, Liam and Ami to school, I would need to pick them up. He was very short with me on the phone and I knew that they were still very angry with me and rightly so.

I spent the day trying to phone James but he just kept rejecting my calls. The only time I heard from him during that day was when he sent me a text message reminding me to pack his clothes and belongings.

After James finished work, he came to collect his things and to give me back his key. I begged him to listen to me, to let me say sorry and to give me one more chance, but he refused. It was over and he was leaving me for good. I had to face the fact that our marriage was really over, I'd destroyed everything, I was devastated and full of regret, but nothing I could do would change his mind.

Chapter 8

Life without James was hard, and I found it incredibly difficult to get used to. The first few weeks were a daze, I was in shock and couldn't really believe he'd left me.

The week after he moved out, James came to see the children every night. The atmosphere was very strange. His first visit, James was still clearly very angry with me and I was still feeling guilty so I was very timid, following him around as he spent time with the children. By the second night though I decided that we couldn't carry on like that so I decided to change my tactics. I'd noticed the night before that he was wearing his best clothes so was obviously on his way to meet his mates, so I thought, "two can play at that game" and put some extra make-up and my good clothes on before he was due to come around.

I asked Luke to let him in and stayed in the kitchen while he talked to the children, waiting for him to come in and say hi to me. I was humming "Oh Blah Dee" as I waited and got to the "life goes on" part just as he walked in. I could tell that he was still a little offhand with me, but as I showed him my new attitude he started to melt a little and we agreed that we needed to be civil with each other for the sake of the children. It was hard enough on them as it was, so we needed to make it as easy as possible. We agreed to try and be friends and after he'd seen the children, he'd come and have a coffee with me.

By the end of the first week, we'd slept together. I was

overjoyed. This meant that he was on the way to forgiving me and that he'd be coming home, but he looked disgusted with himself. He brought me crashing down to Earth telling me that it was just sex and didn't mean anything beside that. I was gutted but determined not to get too upset or worked up. He couldn't possibly mean it, I just had to persuade him that us being together was the right thing to do. I was sure I was right especially because we slept together again the week after that too.

Once we'd broken that barrier, we started to sleep together about twice a week. He'd always repeat himself that it was just sex, but I didn't believe him. We were husband and wife so of course it meant something even if it didn't mean that he was coming home straight away.

The more he said it though, the more it started to hurt me. There were times when I wanted to refuse or push him away. I didn't want to feel used, especially not by my own husband, but I was terrified that if I said no then he'd start to look elsewhere, at least if he was getting sex from me he wouldn't find another woman.

It was so confusing, especially as it was stopping me from moving on properly or being able to grieve the end of our marriage. I felt permanently in limbo.

Financially we were alright. James had always provided for our family and he carried on giving me money every week to make sure we were okay. It was him and the emotional support he gave that I missed the most.

The children missed him terribly too. Liam and Ami were too young to understand what had happened, they only knew that Daddy didn't live with us anymore but Luke understood, and we leaned on each other for support and comfort.

He also took on the role of looking after me as I looked after Liam and Ami. He'd fuss around them to make sure they were okay and listen to me at night if I needed to talk or get things off my chest. He's always been so mature for his age.

One night, while I was putting Liam and Ami to bed, I had a fit. When I came to, I realised that Luke had taken charge. He'd calmed the little ones, called James to let him know that we needed help and then sat with me until I came around. To this day, I get really emotional and proud when I think about how much he helped me back then. He was like my little best friend and I will never forget what he did for us then, and has done for me since.

Even with the children filling the house with laughter I was lonely. I missed James so much that sometimes I found it hard to breathe. I knew that the children missed him too so I'd spend the day making sure they were okay but then find the nights to be torture for me. They'd go to bed and I'd hit the bottle. I'd stopped seeing a lot of my friends and taken to drinking on my own. Most nights I'd just pour myself drink after drink and flick through the television channels; not even paying attention to what was on. Some nights, I'd watch an entire programme but then struggle to remember what I'd watched or what had happened because I'd just zone out.

Because I was bored and upset I'd crash out early and wake up in the early hours of the morning wide awake with the sick feeling in the pit of my stomach all over again.

I carried on like that for weeks, waking early and going through the motions of the day only to sit, drink and cry all night. At least during the day I had the distraction of the children, but at night I had nothing and knowing that James wasn't coming home in the evenings made me start to dread the afternoons too.

Between missing James and then being confused when he was there, I started to drink very heavily. I started to drink the vodka neat and, with every mouthful, I'd feel my problems getting smaller and further away. I'd still sit and cry most nights, but I couldn't feel the tears or the ache in my heart that went with them.

I quickly started to see the vodka as my best friend. As far as I was concerned, that warm liquid was giving me the strength to get through the next day. It was like there was no spark inside me, but drinking brought me to life. What it was actually doing was the exact opposite: it was draining me of all my energy and acting as a depressant it was really making me worse, I just didn't know it at the time.

Of course, the drinking and the whole situation had started to take its toll on my health. I stopped eating because I simply had no appetite, and over the space of about six weeks I lost over two stone in weight. I went from a size sixteen to a size twelve and started getting compliments on how good I looked. A lot of people could see the weight loss but had no idea what was going on and didn't see the broken heart that lay behind the changes. I remember taking the boys to the barbers to get their hair cut and the female barber saying how good I was looking. I felt really embarrassed because I hadn't noticed any difference myself, other than how dreadful I was feeling. I'd get compliments from mums in the playgrounds too. I'd smile and say thank you and wonder how a fake smile and a pair of big sunglasses had managed to fool them into believing I was fine.

When I couldn't stand feeling this helpless any more, I decided I needed to do something and fast, so I went to the doctor for help. They prescribed me some anti-depressants, but they didn't help. I don't really know what I was expecting them to do but I didn't feel any different. I felt just as numb and empty as I had before; all I wanted was a reason to feel alive again. I thought if the tablets could give me the energy to smile then I could turn things around but, as they made no difference, I couldn't find my way out of the rut I'd slipped into. It seemed that my whole life was black and white. I got up and took the children to school, I picked them up, I put them to bed and I drank. And that was it; that was my life. All I wanted was to get through one day without crying and wondering what James was up to that day.

It got so bad that some days I wouldn't even get dressed. If we had no school or visit from James to look forward to then I'd just lounge around the house in my dressing gown all day. The boys would spend the day watching TV or playing on their computers while Ami, who was only about six months old, would be watching the Cbeebies programme on the television or playing with her toys on the floor, and I'd get up when they needed me.

All the while I was taking the pills, I was still drinking and although I had been told that you're not supposed to drink with anti-depressants, it never occurred to me the drinking was the reason they weren't working.

As hard as I was finding things, I knew that the children were suffering too and I knew that with or without the pills and the vodka I wasn't feeling any better. I could see that I was heading for a breakdown and desperately needed a change of scenery and routine.

I'd been speaking to my Nan a lot on the phone. She wasn't as close physically any more as she'd moved to Aberdeen but she knew what had been going on and had been offering as much support as she could. When she asked if we wanted to go up to see her during the holidays I jumped at the chance.

Nan told us all about how she lived near the beach and they had a big fairground for the children. We were all excited and couldn't wait to go, my Nan was amazing and had offered to pay for all of our flights there too. I started to look forward to the trip. I knew that it was just what the kids needed and would make them feel better about what had happened with James, which in itself made me feel better.

As soon as we got there, and I saw Nan, I felt relieved; like a weight had been lifted. The whole situation was just too much to cope with and it was so lovely to see a friendly and familiar face. She was very worried about me and it showed. She just wanted to talk about how I was feeling and after about an hour, we let the children play in her garden while we sat and I told her everything.

I was honest about why things had gone so wrong with James and told her about us sleeping together. I felt I was being used and that it was making me feel worse about the whole thing rather than better. I broke down in tears and told her that my own husband was breaking me and by the end of the conversation she knew everything and was telling me what I already knew about my relationship with James – it was toxic!

We spent two weeks with Nan and although I was still having a drink in the evenings, it wasn't to the same extent that I had at home. I don't know whether it was a conscious effort not to upset or shock Nan or that I simply didn't feel I needed a drink as I had company and something to do, I didn't want to get wasted all the time like I had at home.

I spent so much time with the children, it was great. They were spoiled the whole time we were away and we spent the days at the beach, the fair, shopping, walking around the city and sightseeing, they loved it.

Being able to talk to Nan and get some perspective on the situation meant that I made some decisions too. James had been phoning while we were in Scotland to speak to the children and every time I heard his voice it broke my heart a little more. I knew we couldn't carry on as we were, so I decided that I would go home stronger and be firm with James; I had to tell him that I couldn't cope with the arrangement of "casual sex," if he wanted us back together then it had to be all or nothing.

Whilst we'd been away, James had been making the most of his freedom. As well as going out with his friends, he and Josh had become really close. James moved into the self contained flat in the cellar of his brother's house and was throwing loads of parties. We still had lots of mutual friends who were telling me that he was enjoying the single life and probably wouldn't want to come home to us, but I still had to tell him what I'd decided and what I needed from him. After that it was up to him, but I knew we couldn't carry on as we were.

Nan treated me to some new clothes to go with my slimmer figure before we left her. I stepped back onto the plane much more confident and happier than I had when I arrived, I was determined still that things would have to be different.

The day before we were due to go home James rang to tell me how much he'd missed us all. He asked if he could catch up with the children and sleep over at our house so that he could spend some time with them. I agreed because I knew that we needed to discuss things properly, but I promised myself I wouldn't sleep with him again.

Chapter 9

Rich came to Luton airport to pick us up as James was working. I had a few hours before James was due over, which gave me a chance to unpack and sort things out. I decided to have a drink to calm my nerves and we waited to see the missing member of our family. The children were absolutely thrilled to see their Daddy and they had a lovely time together.

Once we'd got them into bed though, James and I decided to buy some more alcohol and all of my good intentions went out the window. We ended up sleeping together again and, of course, we never had the big discussion I'd planned.

I was furious with myself the next day but I had missed him so much I couldn't help myself. I loved him and longed to be with him which just made not being together even harder.

A few days later, I logged onto our computer. I noticed that James had left his email page open and was still logged in; although I knew it was wrong, I couldn't help but look through his messages.

I was shocked when I saw that there were messages going from James to another girl. I knew who she was too – she was friends with Josh and James, she was even in a relationship herself.

They were definitely flirting with each other and I was completely devastated. There were also messages from James going to his friends and asking if they thought she would be interested in him.

What I remember the most about James leaving us was the physical symptoms it gave me. My heart raced and I felt sick. I was so scared most of the time that when I cried they weren't tears of grief, but those of fear. As I read the messages between James and the girl, those feelings came rushing back, I started to panic and felt short of breath.

I couldn't take it anymore and I rang James for an explanation. He denied that anything was going on with her and that I'd misunderstood. But I knew what I'd read and I was furious. I told him how hurt and used I felt and he came round straight away. He was full of apologies but told me that we weren't a couple anymore and that he could do what he wanted.

I was so upset; James took the children out for a few hours. I wanted, and needed, some time to myself to get things straight in my head. Like he had before, James tried to kiss and cuddle me as he left, but this time I didn't let him and just pushed him away.

I called my friend Maria, and told her what had been happening. She said o cheer me up, we should have a night out on the town that weekend.

Going out with Maria would be the first time I'd gone out in our local town as a single person. By rights I should have been excited, but by that point I was so used to drinking at home and not having to put on any front or pretences that I felt a little nervous, as well as now feeling completely confused by James and the way he was treating me.

James was looking after the children every other weekend but as his place wasn't big enough for all four of them, he stayed with us. That weekend, I was determined that I wasn't going to be used by him again, especially if I'd been out drinking, and I made plans to stay at Maria's whilst he stayed at my house.

In James' absence, I'd also started talking to some of my neighbours. Our local area wasn't very nice and to be honest the people weren't either. There was always a big group of people hanging around the front of the houses, drinking and breaking things and it's no wonder that the area had such a terrible reputation. But I was lonely and I welcomed the friendship.

James arrived early to look after the children while I went on my night out with Maria. To start with, I was moody and offhand with him.

As usual, I had a few drinks before I went out and started to relax a little but then I started downing shots of vodka and my mood changed. I got really upset and James told me he didn't think I was in a fit state to go anywhere.

James wanted me to stay in with him which put me in an impossible situation because that was all that I wanted to do. I got in touch with Maria and made my excuses and stayed at home – all the while my emotions going up and down.

We carried on drinking and the night became a blur. I've had to ask James to fill in this part of the story as I don't remember what actually happened that night.

James told me after a while he thought I'd had enough to drink and should stop. I told him that I was going out after all and there was nothing he could do to stop me. Then I turned and went to walk upstairs to get changed. James tried to stop me by standing between me and the door but that just made me angry.

I turned on him furiously and hit him hard in his head. First on one side; then on the other. He shook me off roughly and as he did I grabbed hold of his arm and bit as hard as I could. He said that I was like a wild animal and that, although he'd seen me in a temper before, I'd never scared him like this.

He shook me away and once I regained my balance, I started to charge towards him again, all the while screaming at him. This time though I was so drunk that I tripped and fell so I grabbed hold of his leg and sunk my teeth into his ankle.

He shouted in pain and I carried on screaming, but suddenly there was a hammering at the door. We assumed that the police had been called, but when we heard lots of shouting we quickly realised that it wasn't the police, but my new found friends… my neighbours!

They'd heard the row and my screaming and assumed that James was attacking me. They were here to stop him, and help me, and they were going to do it physically.

In my rage, I opened the door and let them in. They were carrying baseball bats and there were more of them than usual. I shouted "Get him" and they charged into the kitchen where James was.

As much as I loved James, and as much as I wanted him to want me back, the last few months had hurt. His refusal to commit, feeling like he'd used me for sex and knowing that for the last few weeks he'd been trying to line up my replacement had all taken their toll on me. In the state I was in, I couldn't rationalise and I just wanted him to suffer as much as I had.

I'm horrified by that now, and I'm not trying to make any excuses for what I did that night. It's hard for me to understand the way I was feeling. I know it was very difficult for James to come to terms with after, especially as he's since told me all he wanted was to come home and live with us again, but the amount I was drinking meant he felt completely helpless and unable to.

Going back to that night, James then told me that he started to scream at me to help him, and it sunk in that they were really going to hurt him. That was all I needed to spur me into action and I ran past the mob to stand in between them and James, screaming at them to stop.

Of all of the things I've been told about since becoming sober, this incident scared me the most. Sober, I hate violence. Whether I was causing it or being involved in it; I hate the idea that I hurt people, and when I think about just how much I've hurt James physically as well as emotionally I feel utterly ashamed and devastated.

All I remember is waking up on the sofa the following morning. I felt ill and had a sense of dread creep over me as the blurred memory of what had happened the night before began to pierce its way through.

I was all alone that morning. In the chaos the night before Rich had come to James' rescue and they'd both taken the children to Rich and Jenny's house. Luckily, Liam and Ami had slept through everything and Luke had only just woke up when the neighbours come in. The noise had frightened him and he'd stayed in his bedroom until it died down a little, then come to make sure everyone was okay. By then, the neighbours had gone and James went to talk to him while they waited for Rich, leaving me to cry and eventually pass out.

I hadn't been awake for long when James rang. He was, of course, furious with me and told me that there was no way he was letting the children come back to the house.

Although James had managed to keep a lot of my behaviour from Jenny and Rich while we were together, once we were apart he told them everything. Between the three of them, and other members of the family, they knew that I was an alcoholic and had started to become seriously worried about the children and I.

Chapter 10

It wasn't the first time that James and his family had needed to deal with the fallout of my behaviour, and it wouldn't be the last. Just as they had the night before, many of our arguments would follow the same pattern. I'd drink and he'd tell me I'd had enough. I'd get defensive and upset and he'd beg me to see sense and stop drinking. He'd shout and yell that I was being selfish and that if I could just see what I was and what it was doing to us that I'd stop.

The problem was that I never could. As an addict, help doesn't come to find you. You have to decide to change and nobody can seek help for a problem you don't believe you have. For me, and for many others, alcohol was my friend. It helped me to cope with life and all the problems I felt I had. There was no way I could give it up. I was just lost; so lost that I didn't stand a chance of getting better.

Now in shock, that James had taken the children and wasn't bringing them back, I went straight to the shop to buy a bottle of vodka so that I could think straight. I couldn't believe what had happened – or that I'd let it happen. I started panicking and the more I drank, the more I panicked. I got really drunk, very quickly and decided that I needed to leave the house, but I had nowhere to go. I had nobody I could trust and, of course, I couldn't go to any of James' family.

I decided that the best place for me to go was Luke's grandmothers. Although his dad, Dan and I had split up, Dan's mum had always been nice to me and in my drunken state going to her was a really good plan.

I started to walk but I'd had so much to drink that I got lost and couldn't find my way to her house or back home. I found a phone box and rang Jenny. I lied and told her I'd been attacked and could she get some help for me. She must have known straight away that I was drunk and she soon realised I was lying too. But she kept talking to me, and before I knew it James and Rich turned up.

I couldn't understand at first how they'd managed to find me. Jenny was talking to me and asking questions as to where I was and from my description James had managed to track down the phone box and drove to it as quickly as they could while she kept me on the line.

When he got to me, just as he had been before, James was furious. He shouted at me to get in the car. I refused and started shouting and screaming at him. I had nothing and nowhere to go. I couldn't go home and my life was in a mess, so I was going nowhere. I ran away from James and threw myself onto the floor in the middle of the busy road.

Someone must have seen what was going on because the police turned up. I didn't want to see or talk to anyone though and I ran away again. Thinking they hadn't seen me, I ran down an alley and hid behind a tree but of course, in my drunken state I was nowhere near as stealthy as I imagined. I'd been seen, and they soon found me.

One of the police officers stayed with me, trying to calm me down, while another talked to James. They told James that they would make sure I was okay and get me to a safe place, and that it was probably best for him to go home. They were really nice to me; talking to me calmly and telling me that I didn't have to go anywhere I didn't want to. But they said I needed to find somewhere safe to go while I sobered up.

I had no choice but to do what they were telling me. Of

course, I was too embarrassed to go to any of my friends' houses and have the police deliver me there, and I couldn't go to any of James' family so I decided to stick with my first plan and go to Dan's mums' house. Maggie and her family didn't live too far away and the police agreed to take me there.

It was a crazy idea. Although she'd always been kind to me, we weren't close. I was just so sick of feeling alone and helpless and with everyone turning against me, or at least with me feeling that everyone was out to get me, her house just seemed like a good option.

I was starting to sober up when we arrived and it suddenly hit me that a police car was dropping me off. I just wanted the ground to swallow me – or at the very least, have a blanket for my head so that nobody could see it was me this was happening to.

I sat in the car at first, while the police knocked on Maggie's door and explained the situation. I could see them indicating to me as they asked if I could stay with her until I had sobered up. Maggie agreed and came over to the car. She smiled at me, and asked if I wanted to come in. I was so grateful for the kindness that I started to cry as we walked into the house. Dan's dad, Gavin, and his sister, Gemma were also there and although I hadn't seen them for years, they were lovely to me and looked after me.

I sat and had a coffee with them, after an hour I decided I would be okay to go home. Gavin drove me and came in to make sure I was okay.

When we first walked in, all the smoke alarms were going off and the sound was deafening. Gavin tried to turn them off properly but we thought they must be faulty and he had to hit them hard and eventually break them to get them to be quiet.

Once they'd all stopped, and I could hear myself think, I

realised what a state the house was in. My duvet was on the sofa in a crumpled heap and there were overflowing ashtrays everywhere. The floor was littered with glasses and empty vodka bottles.

Gavin tried to convince me to go back to their house, saying he would come back with me the following morning and help to clean up so that I had somewhere nice to stay and have the children back. I told him I was fine and eventually he left, telling me to contact them if I needed anything.

Once he'd left, I noticed how empty and quiet the house was and I started to cry. I pulled the curtains as I didn't want the neighbours to see inside, or to know I was there. I checked a few bottles and realised they were all empty so I opened my purse. I had a five pound note and a few coppers, just enough for a bottle of cheap vodka. Our smoke alarms sometimes went off because the electricity meter had run out of credit but it never occurred to me to check the electricity. I just wanted to get to the shop so I could buy some vodka. I knew I looked terrible so I found my biggest sunglasses to cover my eyes and hoped I didn't see anyone I knew.

Once I got back, I opened the bottle and started to drink straight out of it. I only did that when things were really bad but as I swilled the vodka down and smoked a few cigarettes I started to calm down. The silence of the house which had been frightening when Gavin first left, now felt calm and comforting. Eventually I started to relax. So much so; that I fell asleep on the sofa.

James came through the back door to avoid any of the neighbours and shook me awake. Had I been sober at this point I might have been frightened or worried about him being there, or just how easy it had been for him to force his way in without waking me up. Because I was still drunk, it never occurred to me to even be concerned.

He was cold with me and just said flatly "Emma, you need help." At the time, he meant psychiatric help. After what had happened, he thought I had mental health problems. I asked what he meant and he told me honestly that he didn't think I was right in the head.

"It's up to you what you do with your life, but the children aren't coming back to this house." He said bluntly.

He'd been uneasy about us being there in the first place because of the areas' reputation, but what had gone on the night previously had really frightened him and he didn't think any of us were safe there. I had no choice in the matter; if I wanted my children living with me then I'd have to find us a new house. He left me to think about what he'd said. Luke, Liam and Ami were to stay with Jenny and Rich until I told him what I was going to do.

I'd called Maria and told her what was going on; with her advice I packed a bag and went over there happy and grateful that she had offered to help. Maria lived opposite our old house where I felt safe and knew the area well; I was relieved I had somewhere to go.

I told her everything; I couldn't cope with James using me, I had nowhere to go with the children, and that I didn't know what to do any more. Then I finally sat down and took off my jacket, Maria saw the bruises on my arms. They were from the night I had attacked James and were self-defence marks from him trying to fend me off but she was shocked, and must have assumed the worst of our relationship. But it wasn't James that started it, it was me.

A little later, I walked down to the shop to buy a bottle of vodka and saw Wendy for the first time in a few months. She asked how I was and her face fell as I told her what had been going on. I showed her my arms and she suggested that I go to a refuge for help.

I didn't know a lot about refuges, but the next day I went to a phone box and called their crisis number. I gave them my side of the story, leaving out how violent I was towards James or how much I was drinking, and they told me that I was experiencing mental and emotional abuse from James. They told me that the best thing for me and the children was a clean break; a new start somewhere safe and away from James because, without the break, neither of us could move on.

Looking back, I feel terrible about the lies I told but I felt that I had no other option. In my head, I hadn't deliberately set out to manipulate anyone. I just needed help to get my children back. Going to the refuge, and allowing them to think my relationship with James was far worse for me was, I thought, the only way I could keep us together. Knowing what I know now about refuges and the women who desperately need those services, I feel utterly terrible about what I did back then.

They told me that they had a room for me, but it would mean a big move for us. The room was in Southend-on-sea in Essex and meant we had to move away from everyone we knew. They informed me that, once we got back on our feet, they would be able to help with re-housing but in the meantime, we just needed to put some distance between James and I.

I called James before I left and asked him to meet me at the house. I told him briefly what I was doing but said I'd explain everything when I saw him.

I was devastated when I got back to the house as I discovered we'd been burgled. The house was completely trashed and had been ransacked. The sofas were slashed, our belongings were gone and even the floor had been ripped up for the copper pipes underneath.

I was horrified and called the police straight away. We

couldn't prove it but I wondered if the neighbours were to blame. The police couldn't do a great deal at the time but took me to the station to give a statement.

James met me at the police station and once I'd finished giving my statement they escorted us back to the house. I was leaving for Southend-on-sea the next morning so we had to pack the house up in the dark. The police stayed outside while we packed our things. James was worried there would be more violence. The electricity had been turned off so the Police Officers even lent us their torches. Being in the house, after what had happened was horrible and we both wanted to get out of there as quickly as possible. James grabbed a sack and packed up the children's clothes and toys while I grabbed all of my things.

Being in the house together gave James and I a chance to talk.

"I'm going to a refuge until I get back on my feet." I told him. "I'll have a key worker and I'll be able to get some counselling."

He looked over at me and said he'd miss me and of course the children once all was settled but he was glad I was finally getting the help I needed.

I should have realised that he thought I was finally seeking help for my state of mind or drinking, but I genuinely thought I was doing what he'd asked, so it didn't occur to me to make sure we were both talking about the same thing.

We decided that the children were going to stay with him until I'd sorted things out properly; I was scared enough about going to the refuge on my own, but I wanted to make sure it was nice and safe for the children first.

Once we'd finished, James drove me to Maria's house. On the way he pulled into the local leisure centre car park and said,

"Come on, we've got time for a last cigarette together."

The whole time we were smoking, both of us were crying. I couldn't believe that it had come to this and I started to feel physically sick. We hugged and as I snuggled into his chest I said.

"I wish I could turn back the clock James and make it work between us."

He held me tight and as he cried he said "I wish we could too."

If I'm completely honest, even if we could turn back time I think my addiction had such a hold of me that although I believed what I was saying, I think I would have made the same mistakes time again. My addiction was the problem, and I was a long way off finding the solution for it. To turn back time would mean to have never opened a bottle.

As James drove away, I felt terrified; I didn't know what my future held – only that James was no longer a part of it.

Chapter 11

I called Diane who ran the refuge, to confirm my arrival and find out which trains I'd need to get there. She gave me all the instructions I needed and told me what to do when I arrived.

James and I planned to meet up in Maidstone town centre the next morning. He was bringing the children so that I could say a proper goodbye to him and them. We met up in Benchley Gardens, a lovely spot where the children knew, we'd taken them there hundreds of times and knew they would feel comfortable and not so scared. It was a huge park that was right next to the train station and had a bandstand where the children would play. We'd taken picnics there before and had many happy memories.

I hadn't seen the children for a few days and I was missing them like crazy. The idea of saying goodbye to them was devastating and although I was trying to keep it together so that they didn't get upset, I worked myself into a terrible state. I saw James first walking towards me holding Liam's hand and pushing Ami's buggy. She saw me and started to cry for me, trying to wriggle her way free while Liam dropped James' hand and ran towards me for a cuddle.

Luke was walking alongside them but didn't rush towards me. He was still furious with me for the night that James had been attacked and I didn't blame him. He'd seen and heard everything and had been terrified by what had gone on. I'd acted disgracefully. What kind of a mother was I?

Knowing how much I'd upset and hurt him only made me more upset and I could see that he was getting into a state too. Luckily, James stepped in and persuaded him to sit down with me for a few minutes. I told him how sorry I was and how much I loved him. We both sat there crying.

Before we knew it, it was time for my train. Liam understood that I was leaving and Ami could sense something was very wrong even though she was very young. They both started screaming and Liam was hanging onto my clothes, trying to stop me from going.

I told James to just go and take them quickly before I changed my mind. He kissed me quickly and picked Liam up to carry him away. I could hear them screaming for me and my heart felt like it would shatter.

With my hands shaking and my heart pounding, I picked up my bags and got onto the train. I purposely chose a seat away from the side of the platform they were walking along and pulled out my sunglasses. I couldn't control the tears any longer and I didn't want anyone to see me.

Because I didn't know what kind of place the refuge was going to be, we hadn't made any plans for James to bring the children to me just yet. The idea that I didn't know when I was going to see them all again was heart-breaking.

I can't remember ever feeling so nervous about going anywhere in my life. I had no idea what to expect, I didn't know anything about refuges, my hopes weren't high and I wasn't expecting it to be a nice place.

I arrived in London Victoria and changed trains; I was now heading towards my new home in Southend. As I watched the platform disappear, I felt sick. I was leaving behind my family and my husband to go to a strange place, and I had no idea what my future would be. I tried to stay calm, but the tears streamed, I was thankful I had my glasses on. I didn't think I could cope if anyone asked me what was wrong.

The journey took an hour from London and I spent the whole time looking out of the window. Soon I could see the sea. I felt a little calmer and more hopeful that I was doing the right thing. The hour passed very quickly and before I knew it I was there.

When I came out of the station, I saw a shop opposite and popped in to get a soft drink and a snack to take with me. I walked to the top of the road and found the refuge. I don't really know what I was expecting, but it just looked like a huge house. It was a little run down and looked like it needed a lot of love.

I was nervous as I rang the bell. Diane answered the door and instantly put me at ease. She introduced herself as the manager and took me into her office. She informed me we needed to go over the ground rules, complete some paperwork and discuss any issues and then she would take me for a tour and show me to my room.

Diane's kindness and the welcome she gave me was enough to make me crumble and I finally broke down. As I cried, she reassured me and went through the rules asking if I had any drug or alcohol issues too as there was help available if I did. Of course, I foolishly said no.

At that moment, I knew deep down I had a problem.

I'd tried on occasions to stop drinking in the past. I'd make the decision to stay sober for one night and would set myself the challenge. Those nights were horrendous. I'd snap at the children for the slightest thing, working myself up into a foul mood over anything and everything. Eventually I'd decide that I couldn't carry on and blame the stress of whatever was going on and make an excuse, partly for myself and partly for anyone who would listen, I'd give in and open a bottle. I'd always say that I just needed a small one to keep myself going, but that would go down too nicely or quickly and before I knew it, I'd broken my resolve and bought a full bottle.

I wasn't trying to lie to Diane, or to deliberately lead her on. I knew that if I told her I had a problem right then, she'd try to make me stop just like James had, and I couldn't cope with the thought of stopping right then, inside I was already desperate for a drink.

Luckily, she didn't try to press the issue. We had a quick chat while I filled out the forms and then she showed me around.

My room was on the ground floor and had a shared bathroom opposite. Diane had arranged for my room to be made up ready and had left a basket on my table filled with food, hairbrushes and other essentials. She explained that many women arrived with nothing and no money to buy those things, and she hadn't known what I'd be bringing with me. They receive donations of food and she said if I needed anything else I should let her know.

The room was pretty and bright and I felt at home. Under a window in the corner was a single bed with a yellow and white chequered duvet cover. Opposite was a TV on the wall and a built-in wardrobe, I had a little kitchen with a sink, microwave, toaster and cupboards.

Once we'd seen my room, Diane took me on a tour of the rest of the house. There were three floors with fourteen other bedrooms, a shared laundry room, a big playroom and a garden which had toys and benches. Aside from the bedrooms, which were of course invitation only, I could use any of the facilities.

I told Diane about my children and that eventually I wanted to live with them again. She suggested that I spent my first weekend getting used to the house and making sure it was somewhere I wanted to bring the kids to, and then we could talk again on Monday to re-evaluate.

Diane gave me an emergency number I could use to contact her if needed and said the other women staying at the house had gone out for the afternoon to the beach. She assured me they were a friendly bunch and would look after me.

Then she left and I was alone. Once she'd gone, I went back to my room, lay down on the bed and cried.

I stayed there crying and feeling sorry for myself for a while. After such a gut wrenching day, I just wanted to sob my heart out. The release did me the world of good but I knew if I stayed there then I wouldn't want to leave. I headed outside for a cigarette and met some of the women who had returned from the beach, the garden felt busy with a few of them there. A little overwhelmed I shyly introduced myself and was thrilled to find that Diane was right: they were a lovely bunch; though there were too many names to remember!

They said I shouldn't stay in my room and to come and be sociable. They invited me to join them in the garden later that evening too, and made me feel very welcome. It was such a relief having felt so anxious all day about what I was walking into.

I made a lot of friends at the refuge. Everyone had their own reasons for being there and some of them were horrific. I felt a lot better around them, a little safer and very relieved but I was really missing my children and was still terrified about what the future held. I rang James to tell him I'd arrived safely and spoke to all of the children individually. Hearing their voices and knowing they were okay made me feel better and I started to calm down, but I was missing them terribly and wished I could just hold them in my arms.

That night I ventured into the garden for a smoke and was determined to get to know the girls a little better. I wanted to make the most of the situation. I met three girls that night;

Lisa, Jackie and Karla. They were lovely and they pulled out a chair for me, letting me join in their conversation.

They pointed out a little shed in the corner and explained that although alcohol was banned in the house, many of them kept it in the shed as they liked a drink in the evening. They warned me that the staff did random house checks, so I would have to hide any booze and make sure any bottles I'd used were thrown away, and out of the house the next day.

I hadn't brought any vodka with me as I didn't know if it was allowed and I didn't want to break the rules on my first night. In any event, I was exhausted from the day and just needed to sleep, so as a rare occasion I went to bed sober and physically drained.

I didn't sleep particularly well but still felt much better the next morning; I was excited and wanted to explore the area of my new home. I asked some of the girls for the local train and bus routes and set off. As I walked off the platform and onto the road I saw the beach right in front of me. I sat for about an hour watching the waves, I found it really calming and relaxing, once I felt ready, I went for a stroll around the town.

I found the feeling of knowing that I wouldn't bump into anyone I knew very freeing and Southend really was a lovely place. I knew there and then that the four of us could have a lovely new start here, and for the first time in a long time I didn't feel so scared about the distance I was putting between myself and James.

I had a lovely day, followed by a brilliant night. I went into the garden with the girls again. This time though I decided to join in with them and took a bottle of vodka. We swapped stories and I found that my new friends were really supportive.

I told them all about James and how he'd left me but wouldn't leave me alone. I didn't want my new friends to think badly of me so I left out a lot about my drinking and the rows we'd had. Again, I wasn't trying to manipulate the situation; I genuinely did believe that James' behaviour amounted to mental torture, and when they started to share their stories about violent or emotionally abusive partners, I put James in the same category even though he didn't belong there.

After a drink and the conversation, I was exhausted again, returned to my room and fell into a deep sleep. I was glad of the drink that night, for the first time I was starting to notice the quietness of my bedroom. The main parts of the refuge were hectic and busy, with loud chatter and children giggling or crying but once I got back into my room alone I had time to think and that's when it hit me just how much I missed the children. At least the vodka knocked me out enough to numb the pain.

I woke up without any plans to do anything. With the empty silence looming, I knew I had to leave the refuge, even if it was just for a walk. I realised how much I needed the children with me. Our future was here and it involved just me and my children. By the time I'd come back from my walk, I'd decided that, the next time I saw her, I'd tell Diane that I needed to be with the children and see if she could do something to help me.

There was an empty room upstairs and I spent the whole weekend hoping and praying that there wouldn't be any emergency admissions as I thought the room would be perfect for the four of us.

With a plan in my head, I went out into the garden and found Karla having a smoke. Karla didn't have any children and just like me she didn't have any family to rely on either. We spent the day outside talking and getting to know each other better. During the chattering, we decided to go out that night. We had barely any money, but we weren't about to let that stand in our way.

I hadn't really appreciated how much weight I'd lost but that night I dressed up and really made an effort. Karla and I had a brilliant night, guys were flirting with us and were buying us drinks all night. We weren't interested in any of them but we didn't turn the drinks down!

Although the night itself was brilliant, neither of us had thought about how we'd get home and we were shocked to find out the price of the taxi back to the refuge. By the time we left the club it was almost four in the morning. We discovered the trains would be running again in a few hours so we walked down to the beach to watch the sun come up. The sunrise was beautiful and we both felt very peaceful at the end of a great night. We headed home, tired but happy.

I slept in until late morning and when I finally got up Diane called me into her office. She wanted to introduce me to Sally who would be my key worker. Every person staying at the refuge had their own key worker who was responsible for making sure they had everything they wanted at the home, as well as access to counselling, social services and any other support they needed. Sally and her colleagues were employees of the charity who ran the refuge and they were based there all the time in case we needed something.

Once we'd been introduced, Sally asked me if there was anything I needed from her. She told me about the services she could refer me to and asked if I had a plan for my future. I told her how much I was missing the children and that now I was sure of the house and the area I really wanted them to come and live with me as soon as possible. The empty room I'd seen must have already been earmarked for somebody as I wasn't offered it, but Sally did tell me that she would try to find a bigger room for me and the children. She apologised as she couldn't guarantee how long it would take or that we would be able to stay in the same home. Nevertheless I felt happier knowing that the wheels were in motion to get my children back.

The following weekend James' Dad brought the children to see me. Things were still tense between us but he told me that he would leave me with the children and meet us back by the train station in a few hours.

I was overjoyed to see them and we had a wonderful time together. I showed the children around the local area and we went to the beach. There was a pirate show and we all sat down to watch and have some lunch together. I was determined to impress Luke and I was thrilled when he told me that he loved Southend-on-sea and would be really excited to come and live there. I was thrilled and although Liam and Ami were too young to really understand, they seemed happy and contented which was enough for me to know that this was right for all of us.

At the end of a lovely day, it was time for the children to go. Rich was waiting but gave us a chance to cuddle and say goodbye properly. Saying goodbye to them was devastating for me all over again, as well as for them.

Luke was quiet as he knew what was coming but Liam and Ami couldn't understand and got so upset that I found it hard to keep it together. Once they'd left with Rich, I went for a walk to try and clear my head. Although I was upset at them leaving, having a plan in place to get them back meant that it wasn't as hard for me as when I'd initially moved away.

I'd been staying in touch with James and as much as he loved having the children, he was finding it a struggle. There wasn't enough room for him to stay with Jenny and Rich so they were all staying in Josh's basement flat which was small and cramped. James agreed that once we'd got the arrangements made, he would return them to my care where they'd have space and freedom.

When I arrived back to the refuge that night I was much happier. Our drinks in the garden were starting to become a nightly thing now and I was really enjoying the company of the other girls. I started to think of them as proper friends.

For as long as I could remember, I hadn't felt that I'd had any support. Without my own family around me, I'd felt scared and lost whenever I'd had a bad day, but the girls in the refuge welcomed me in as one of them and made me feel warm and protected again. For the first time in a long time, I was starting to feel positive.

A few days later, I was overjoyed when Sally called me into the office and told me that one of the bigger rooms upstairs was due to become free in the next few days, and that if I wanted it for me and the children it was ours.

I rang James straight away and he agreed that the children could come and live with me. A few days later, James brought the three of them to see me. It was Luke's birthday and I paid for the four of us to have a treat. As much as I loved seeing the children, seeing James again was strange. He was very affectionate; kissing and cuddling me again. I just didn't understand what he wanted from me and as much as I still loved and missed him, I knew that I had to move on. I knew by that stage that we had no future as a couple and I couldn't see the point in confusing myself and letting myself get hurt again.

The children moved into the refuge with me the following week. It had been a whole month since I'd last spent a night with them, it had felt like torture living without them and I was so delighted to have them back.

The new room was huge and we had our own kitchen, dining table and bunk beds for us to sleep in. Lots of the other women also had children and they quickly made friends. I managed to get Luke into a local school and Liam started at a local playschool. Ami seemed content being at home all day with me, and so they settled in straight away.

The refuge arranged for us to register with the local doctor and on my first visit our new doctor was very pro-active, he noticed from my records that I was midway through the tests for the fits I'd been having but had missed appointments. He quickly arranged to re-start the process.

James would take the children to stay with him every other weekend, and when it was my weekend off Karla and I would go into town together.

I was also enjoying my social life in the garden and spent every night out there once I'd put the children to bed. The refuge was used by a lot of people as a stop gap while they sorted out their next move and so lots of girls came and went, but everyone who came to stay was lovely and I felt settled for the first time in a long time. I was also feeling as though I could be happy without James.

Of course, James and I were still friends and we still talked regularly. I'd stopped putting kisses at the end of text messages and although I knew that I still loved him, I wasn't upset any more. The distance between us and the fact that I only saw him briefly when he picked the kids up was helping me move on.

I was feeling happy and looking forward to a night out with Karla, I found a little black dress in the sales for five pound. I was loving my new slimmer figure now and felt really good about myself, it was so nice to treat myself and it made me feel good.

Karla and I were up for a good night that weekend, and we headed to my favourite club. We had a brilliant night and towards the end of the night a man approached me, he introduced himself, flirted a little and I felt flattered. After separating from James, I hadn't wanted to look at another man. I was married and that was it for me. But after all this time it was nice to have a little attention.

Gregg was quite drunk and was practically begging me to dance with him, I was with my friend and I didn't want to leave her, I'd learnt from so many mistakes and so I politely refused. I gave him my number but I didn't really expect to hear from him again. I was over the moon when he called the next day.

He didn't live very far from the refuge. I told Gregg the full situation about the refuge and the children and he didn't seem to be put off, so we arranged to meet up again soon.

The following night I got really drunk with the girls outside and Gregg and I started to text each other. Drunk on vodka, the flirtatious attention, I decided I wanted to see him. The kids were safely in bed so I asked Lisa to keep an eye on them for me and went to meet Gregg at the top of the road.

Although I was already really drunk, once Gregg and I had said hello we went straight to the shop, bought some drinks and went and sat on the bench outside. We were chatting and flirting as well as drinking a lot. As it got late, it got colder and colder and we started to huddle together.

When Diane had first welcomed me to the house, she'd made it clear that one of the main and most important house rules was that no men were allowed. The rule made sense as many of the women and families they supported were escaping abusive and violent relationships.

Although I could still hear her warning ringing in my ears, my drunken brain decided to ignore it and I asked Gregg to come home with me. It was late, I didn't think that any of the other girls would be awake and I was sure he could sneak out before any of them woke in the morning.

My children were asleep in our room so I took Gregg downstairs into the communal lounge and we started to kiss. Things were just going a little further when Jackie walked in.

Jackie was disgusted with me and gave me a horrible look before storming back to her room. I knew that I'd made a huge mistake and asked Gregg to leave. We agreed to call each other the next day and I could feel myself beginning to fall for him.

The next morning was horrible. Jackie had told the other girls what I'd done and they were angry with me. They had every right to be – I'd put everyone's safety at risk by bringing a strange man back to somewhere they were supposed to be safe and secure. I've done a lot of stupid things while drunk, but putting all of them in danger like that is one of the most dangerous and selfish.

Faced with all of the angry girls, I did what I'd always done and ran away from the problem. I dropped the boys off at school and took myself and Ami out for the day while I worked out what to say to them.

When I returned, I had a few swigs of vodka in my room. I knew alcohol was forbidden in the house, but when you're an addict you find ways to hide your stash. I had to be careful as a few girls had been found with alcohol and given a warning. Three warnings and you were out!

Keeping a secret stash was relatively easy though, I was always careful with my bottles and would keep them along with my mints and perfume, to disguise the smell in my handbag which was with me at all times.

That night, I needed a few drinks before I faced the girls in the garden. I knew I'd behaved badly but I also knew I needed to see them as it would only get worse if I hid myself away.

I think they all realised I had a drink problem. Nobody ever said anything to me, but I could tell by the looks they were giving me and the way they acted that they'd realised I wasn't as together as I'd tried to have them believe. They were very angry with me and after that day a lot of them started to keep their distance. I'd managed to alienate everyone and I only had myself to blame again.

Jackie was the only person who actually discussed what happened with me. She told me how angry she was, she felt I'd let them all down. I knew she was right so I didn't even try to defend myself; all I could do was apologise. She agreed she wouldn't take it any further and I was very grateful to her for that.

Everyone seemed to take the same view as Jackie. They were angry but we dealt with it among ourselves without involving any of the staff. I would have definitely been thrown out, but after what I'd done nothing was ever the same again. Their opinions of me had changed and there was nothing I could do to make it right.

I carried on texting Gregg throughout the week and decided it was time to tell James. I felt that even though we were finished, I owed it to him to tell the truth. I thought I was being respectful towards him as we were still married. But in a way I hoped he would feel the same jealousy and longing that I'd felt when I'd seen the messages on his computer.

I sent him a text message telling him that I'd met someone else and that I was moving on. Five minutes later, I was shocked when I got a reply with a kiss at the end!

Soon after that, James called me. He said that he still loved me and that my text had made him realise just how much. He said he was coming to see me so that we could talk things through.

Emily had just moved into the refuge and wasn't aware of the Gregg incident. She offered to babysit while I went to meet James. My heart skipped a beat, a little excited and pleased that I obviously still meant something to him.

We went to a bar in town to talk. I knew I still loved him but

I had to be honest with myself and told him that I just didn't how we could work things out. James was still in Kent and I was in Southend.

With James in one county and me and the children in another, it seemed like a hopeless situation but James told me that he was prepared to leave Kent and start a new life with us in Southend. He said my text had really made him think, and he was ready to give us one last chance.

I practically jumped into his arms. As much as I liked Gregg, I loved James and although we'd been through hell in the last few months none of that love had gone away. I also knew that being with their Daddy was the best thing for the children too. They had missed him so much and needed to be back with him, just like I did.

Over the next few weeks, James and I worked on building our relationship. We stayed in hotels and things were fantastic between us. The kids were absolutely over the moon with us back together again. Although I couldn't tell anyone yet, my future was clear for the first time in a long time – with my husband and my children at the centre of it.

Chapter 12

As much as I was excited for our new start, I found that it wasn't as easy as I'd hoped to find a new home for all of us.

The refuge had been a huge help, but with all four of us living in the one room, it was really crowded, and none of us had any privacy. James obviously couldn't live with us, so we had to move out. I spoke to the local council but they told me there was a long waiting list and it could take quite some time before a house big enough for all of us became available.

They suggested we looked at private landlords. However, there was a problem with that idea too: I would have to find money for a deposit, which I didn't have.

As much as this was an obstacle, I couldn't see the harm in looking at a few houses to see what was available and, of course, I fell in love! The first house I looked at was just a few minutes away from the refuge and it was home at first sight! It had three big bedrooms, a lovely bathroom, a lounge and a separate dining room. But best of all, there was a huge garden where the children could play.

The house was within walking distance from Luke's school, he had settled in really well and I didn't want to move him again. Liam was also due to start at the same school in a few weeks so the house was absolutely perfect for us.

The only problem was the deposit and I was terrified that by the time we managed to find the money the house would be long gone. Luckily, we still had my Nan to help us and she said that she would pay the deposit for us as long as I promised to look after the house. That way, when we decided to leave she would still get the deposit back. I was scared to tell my Nan that James and I were back together and that he'd be living with us. I didn't want to worry her after all of the things I'd said about our break up and I was also worried that she wouldn't approve. So I kept it a secret for a little longer. James and I were still sneaking around seeing each other in secret. We were finding it harder and harder and of course it didn't help that we were paying for hotels every weekend just so that we could spend time together, that money would have really helped towards our deposit and new home, but there was no other way to spend time together while I was in the refuge.

The children would always come with us and we'd treat our little hotel breaks like mini holidays, making the most of our time together after so much time spent apart. I remember that one of the nicest nights we had was in a hotel on Southend seafront. The hotel was pretty and really reasonably priced, so we'd booked in and had been astounded when they showed us our room. It was a full suite with two bedrooms; the children had a single bed and a double, and through an adjoining door there was a room for James and I. Best of all, there was a door to a balcony where we could sit and watch the sea.

Once we'd settled into the room, we went for a walk along the seafront and bought the children fish and chips for supper. As we walked back, we noticed there was a festival on with some great bands, we stood and watched a few of them play while the children tired themselves out dancing.

James had told me from the start that he would only come back and let us try again on the condition that I wouldn't drink. I was fine with that; I knew it was either James or the drinking and I desperately wanted the children to have their family back together, I was looking forward to having my own house again with a normal life.

Finally, the day came when I had to say goodbye to the refuge, it was much harder than I expected. When I first arrived I was broken; but thanks to the family I found there I was strong and confident when I left. In such a short space of time, I'd changed and grown much stronger, as well as making some good friends. I owed them so much, and on the day I left I got really emotional.

From the burglary in Maidstone we'd lost a lot of our belongings, what hadn't been stolen had been ruined. Stupidly, we hadn't been insured, so we'd lost everything and would need to start afresh as we moved into our new home. I suppose I should have been scared, but, in truth, I was so excited about us all being reunited that what might have been worrying was actually like a little adventure.

Despite us not having much in the way of belongings, the house was ready for us to move straight into. The garden was designed especially for children: it had a swing set, see-saw and a trampoline which the previous tenants had left. Luke, Liam and Ami were in heaven.

The kitchen was fully fitted with a fridge, freezer and a cooker. The only thing it didn't have was a washing machine, but I was happy to hand-wash all of our clothes for the time being.

The refuge was used to people leaving with very little and they had given us two televisions and some other essential items. I had a little bit of money saved up and James went out and bought some beds and a three-piece suite. We knew it would be a while before we were properly settled, but I couldn't wait for us to be a family in our very own home again.

My Nan came down from Aberdeen on the day we moved as she needed to sign all the Guarantor forms and helped us move out of the refuge. She stayed with me and the children for a few days, helping us to get settled, she thought the house and the area were lovely and I was pleased she like it.

Although I still hadn't told her that James and I were back together, he was there on moving day. I told her he had come to see the children and help us to get settled, but I'm sure that she must have had her suspicions about what was really going on.

Once Nan had gone home, it was time for James to move in with us. Although the children and I were very excited, James was having a very stressful time. His family were dead set against him moving in and us getting back together, they wouldn't help him so he had to do everything on his own. By the time he arrived at the house, he was stressed and really upset at having to say goodbye to his life and family in Maidstone – both of which he adored.

Christmas was just around the corner, and as a special treat I'd promised the children that on moving day we could go and see the Christmas lights being switched on in town. James arrived just as we were due to go out and although he seemed tense I told myself it was just the move and he would be fine. We had a great time and it seemed that everything was perfect.

For the first few weeks things were fine. I stuck to my promise and didn't drink at all. It was hard and the cravings were awful at times. I was stressed, irritable and very emotional all the time. I'd lose my temper or cry over the slightest thing and I knew it was my craving for alcohol to blame. At the time, I'd never spoken to a doctor about my problem and I didn't believe I was an alcoholic so it didn't even enter my head to approach a support group like Alcoholics Anonymous. I knew by now that I had a problem with alcohol but I wasn't ready to admit it to anyone else and didn't fully understand the seriousness of my addiction; so I carried on alone trying to manage the problem myself. But I became moodier and more stressed by the day. I'd made James a promise and I was determined to stick to it.

As well as finding it hard to manage without a drink, we were also finding things very difficult financially. James had to give up his job in Maidstone to move to Southend. We'd hoped that he'd find a new job quickly, but sadly things didn't happen that easily, it was almost Christmas and companies don't tend to take on new staff around that time. We struggled to cope on benefits alone and the financial stresses didn't do our relationship any favours, as a result we started to argue again.

We put all the fights aside for Christmas Day and had a really lovely day. James cooked us all a big dinner and we made the day all about the children. I could tell that James was missing his own family though, especially as he always saw them at Christmas. His parents were still unhappy about us being together and they were missing the children like crazy, so James arranged for him and the children to go to their house on Boxing Day. There was never any question of me joining them, but to be honest I was okay with that.

After such a crazy few weeks, I was looking forward to having a bit of time to myself. I was still in touch with Karla from the refuge and as she was spending Christmas alone, we arranged to meet up while James was with his family.

We planned to go to Mayhem for a post-Christmas party. I decided not to tell James, as I knew he wouldn't want me to go, but as he was away and I had been so good at not drinking, I decided I'd earned it. I told myself that a few drinks and a little fun wouldn't hurt anyone.

I'd arranged with Karla to stay at her house for the night. She'd just moved into her own home and it was really close to the town so taxis would be cheap too. I treated us both to a pizza before we went out, thinking that if I'd eaten properly then I shouldn't have a hangover when James got back the next day.

Being out and drinking again felt really great and my good intentions were soon out of the window. Karla and I were having a great night and I soon started downing shots as well. It's frightening how quickly I got lost in the moment. As the end of the night drew closer, Karla and I were sitting down when Gregg came over to us. I had finished things with him with just a text message but he told me he had lots he wanted to tell me, so I figured there was no harm in just talking to him. He bought us a drink and I sat with him for a while, talking and eventually kissing!

I was so drunk by that stage that I left Karla in the club, alone, and took Gregg back to my house. I'd left my keys at Karla's house so I asked him to smash the porch window. I knew I was going to have to explain what had happened to the landlord but because of the amount I'd had to drink the broken window just seemed like an inconvenience; I thought I could deal with it in the morning.

The next morning I woke up, sober, with Gregg. I couldn't remember anything but it was obvious that I'd slept with him. I started to panic and knew that I had jeopardised my family again. Gregg could tell how panicked I was and said he was leaving.

I just kept telling him I was sorry, that I loved James and sleeping with him was a huge mistake.

I went downstairs to let him out and with a sickening lurch saw the broken window. Memories started to flood back and I realised just what I'd done. Gregg told me that he would go home to get changed and come back to help me; in the meantime I tried desperately to figure out what to do.

The only money I had was the landlords rent money, but this

was an emergency and I had to fix the window before James and the children came back. I was hung-over and really suffering, as well as feeling very emotional and guilty.

I went out to find a piece of glass and luckily managed to get the size I needed, then I headed home to wait for Gregg. After a while it became obvious that he wasn't coming back and I was on my own in a mess: James could be back any time soon and I needed to think fast.

Later that night when James arrived home I told him that Karla had met a man in the club and left me. I had nowhere to stay and no choice but to break into our house. Luckily he believed me but I could tell he wasn't happy with me at all, especially as I hadn't told him that I was going out. He told me that whenever I went out there was some sort of drama. He quickly let it go and we had a nice time for the rest of the Christmas holidays.

We carried on still struggling for money and still worrying about how we'd cope. The lack of a job seemed to really hit James and he started to get more and more depressed. Eventually he found a little work collecting charity bags. It was a simple idea; James would post an envelope through people's door with a plastic bag inside. He'd indicate on the envelope that he'd be back in three days to collect their filled bag with donations of clothes, shoes and blankets for the charity. James then took the bags back to the depot and be paid for what he'd collected based on the weight of the bags, so the more he collected the more he'd get paid. James was good at the job, and although it didn't pay fantastically well, it gave him something to get up in the morning for.

Now in our new home, I'd received a letter from Kings College Hospital inviting me for a scan. James took me for the scan and as much as I hated it and felt very claustrophobic again, I knew it was for the best so I tried to relax and let them get it over and done with as fast as possible.

A few days later, as promised, I received my results. I wasn't expecting them to have found anything and so I wasn't feeling too nervous about opening my letter. But when I did, I had to sit down and read it through several times.

The letter explained that a slow growing tumour had been found. It was located in the left Hippocampus of my brain. I kept seeing the word tumour and feeling the blood rush to my head while the strength left my legs.

I shouted for James and tried to continue with the rest of the letter through my tears. I read that the tumour had probably always been there and was most likely benign but that didn't alleviate my fear.

James read through the letter, and although he managed to calm me down a little, I could tell it had rattled him too. He called our doctors surgery and made an appointment for the following morning.

In shock we just sat there, unsure what to say or do.

We showed our new doctor my letter, she already had a copy along with additional information from the scan and she patiently explained everything to us.

Apparently this type of tumour was very common and as long as it proved to be benign then it could be controlled with tablets. She informed me that they were ninety percent certain it would be benign, this was a relief but I was still concerned. She wrote me a prescription to start the medication immediately but explained the hospital would review all of my medication when I met with the Consultant.

She was very kind and told me not to worry. It was practically impossible to do anything but worry but with at least three weeks to go until my appointment with the Consultant, there wasn't really anything else I could do.

My hospital appointment came through about two weeks later

and James came with me again. This time I was terrified. I was shaking and sweating and completely focused on the tumour. I felt so sure they were going to say I was seriously ill or that it was the "Big C" that I started to cry in the waiting room. The wait seemed to take forever but finally they called my name and we went into the Consultant's office.

He sat me down and started to explain about the tumour. He showed me the screen on his computer. There was a picture of my brain, he showed me where the tumour was and that this area was used for memory.

I started to get worked up again and as he carried on talking, I was growing more and more impatient. Finally, I couldn't wait any longer. I had to know what it all meant and he was taking far too long to get to the point.

"Is it cancerous?" I asked quietly, hardly daring to say the word cancerous.

"No" he said as my heart leapt. I started to cry with relief and he began to explain that although they didn't think the tumour would even carry on growing, they would continue scanning every so often and I would have to take the medication for the rest of my life.

He referred me to a specialist clinic to explain how to manage my condition.

It was such a relief to hear I didn't have cancer that when I was told I would have to manage my condition for the rest of my life with medication it simply felt like a huge weight had been lifted.

We faced more problems when the insurance expired on our car because James' job was miles away. We had no choice but to keep running it. We couldn't afford to reinstate the insurance without the work, and James couldn't work without the car, so we took the risk of no insurance and hoped for the best.

Of course, our luck wouldn't hold and one day James rang me in tears. He'd been stopped by the police who had seized the car. He was stranded miles away with no car and no money. We had no choice but to ring his family and beg them to help. Just like we knew he would, Rich dropped everything to pick him up and brought him home looking broken. Of course losing our car meant that we'd lost our income too and we were back to square one with a fine for having no insurance on the car looming over us too.

Again we tried to pick up the pieces and as the weeks went on both of us sank lower and lower into debt and depression with no end in sight. Weeks went by and James carried on looking for work until one day Josh called him. The whole family were worried about James and Josh was calling to offer him a full time job working in Josh's shop back in Maidstone. I was convinced James wouldn't accept, but he did! I was both furious with him and devastated, but James knew he had to take the job and was determined to keep the family together even though he wouldn't be living with us. He said he would come to visit every weekend.

I was gutted and begged him not to leave. Deep down I was just so hurt and felt rejected, it seemed that his leaving was the end of us all over again.

Chapter 13

James lived up to his promise and came home every weekend. I didn't drink at all at weekends, but during the week I was lonely and quickly fell back into my old routine drinking every night. What started out as a quick drink to calm my nerves after a busy day; quickly became a half bottle of vodka every night. I would have drunk more but as money was so tight, I had to limit myself.

I was expecting to be lonely but instead saw lots of my friends during the week. Karla had forgiven me for leaving her at the club and we would get together once a week at my house and always have a good night. She started work shortly after leaving the refuge and had to get up early so she would stay over and I'd wake her in the morning when I woke the children up for school and we'd walk out together.

One night she brought her friend Vicky with her. She too had lived in the refuge but left before I arrived. She had a little girl called Clara who was the same age as Ami, and the girls played well together. We quickly became good friends, drinking and taking the children to the beach in the evenings.

As much as I was enjoying my new freedom, I hated the fact that James had left us. His family had been so against us being back together, and for him to leave us and go back to them at the first sign of trouble felt like a double betrayal. He had abandoned us; the way I saw it was that he'd chosen his family over our relationship and the children. What I didn't see was that he was simply working away from home to make ends meet like so many other families do.

But then I found out through a mutual friend that he was telling his family we'd separated again, apparently it was keep the peace with them. I was furious with him and very hurt. After only just being able to forgive him for all of the months I'd felt he was using me for sex, I felt as if any trust or love I had for him had been soured. I didn't even think about some of my actions in the past.

As far as I was concerned, he should have stayed with me in Essex and we should have found a solution together, but his answer had been to run away again. So while I seethed at James, I found solace in my friends.

Vicky came round to mine one night with some news, although she was in a relationship, she was also getting text messages from another man. She told me that she wasn't interested in him, but the messages kept coming.

It was about a week later when I met the man she was talking about. Vicky and I had taken the children to a local pub. We went to The Eagle quite often as there was a playground for the children and it had a nice atmosphere.

We were sitting outside when Vicky suddenly groaned and put her head in her hands. I was worried and asked her what was wrong. The guy had just arrived at the pub with his friend. He came over to our table and she introduced Mark to me.

I expected Vicky to want to leave straight away, but we ended up staying and surprisingly having a nice afternoon with them.

The next weekend James had been due to come home, but I decided I wanted some time to myself and asked if he would just pick the children up and take them away to his family for the weekend. I felt so angry with him that I had weekends where I felt too tired to keep up the pretence that all was well.

James agreed and picked the children up on the Saturday. Once he'd left, Vicky came round and we spent the rest of the night drinking. Vicky was one of the few friends I had at the time who didn't really drink – but she didn't mind me drinking.

As the evening went on and I got drunker and drunker Vicky kept getting text messages from Mark. In my drunken state, I thought it would be funny to text him. I told myself that Vicky didn't like him and I fancied having some fun so I sent him a message from me. He replied quickly saying that he remembered me and liked me too. We carried on sending text messages all night and eventually, as I often did in my drunken state, I invited him to come over.

Vicky went home a little later and I think she was secretly pleased that I'd shown an interest in Mark. She'd just started seeing someone she really liked so she definitely wasn't interested in him.

I'd told her my half of the story with me and James and like many of my friends at the time, she'd been telling me that she thought James was no good for me and that it was time I moved on.

After Vicky left, I was planning on going to bed when there was a knock on the door. It was Mark, with a very big bottle of vodka in his hand. Of course I welcomed him in and we started on the vodka straight away. One thing led to another and we ended up in bed.

I was used to waking up with regrets but this was one morning when I didn't. We really liked each other and arranged to meet up again the following weekend when he was home on leave from the army. He gave me something to look forward to. I realised later while I was tidying up that he'd left a key behind. I messaged him to let him know and said I'd keep it safe until I saw him next.

As angry as I was with James, I didn't want to go behind his back. I knew that we couldn't carry on as things were and the next day I made a decision: I had to end things with him. It didn't go well. I told James I was sorry but I'd met somebody else, he was angry and upset. That didn't change my mind though – in my eyes James had made his decision, I'd been telling him for weeks how unhappy I was with him living away from us and he'd had the chance to put things right. As far as I was concerned, it was his own fault.

The following week was horrible; James and I did nothing but exchange nasty text messages, followed by him ringing me in tears begging me to change my mind. But it was too late – I just didn't want to know anymore.

All the while, Mark and I were sending flirtatious messages to each other and I felt really happy. He wasn't sure if he'd be back the following weekend and asked if his cousin Ken could collect the key. I said that was fine and waited for Ken to appear. I hadn't met him before but I could tell straight away when he knocked on the door that he and Mark were related. They both had a similar shaped face, and just like Mark, he had a friendly smile. He took the key and went on his way and I hardly gave him another thought.

A few days later, I was in the local paper shop and the girl who worked behind the counter started to talk to me. Her name was Rachel and although I only knew her through the shop, she was always friendly.

With a huge grin on her face, she told me that she'd heard about me and Mark. I was a little shocked but she told me she was good friends with Ken and that he'd told her. We got chatting and had a laugh about the whole thing. I went back to the shop later on for my nightly bottle of vodka and Rachel was still there. I asked if she was doing anything later that night and invited her over. She asked if it was okay for her to bring Ken and another friend, as I preferred to have company than be on my own I agreed and hurried home to get the children ready for bed.

I still didn't feel comfortable with new people unless I'd had a drink, so before everyone arrived I quickly downed the bottle I'd just bought. It was my normal nightly bottle which was a half-litre, but I still had butterflies and wished I had more. I'd just finished when the bell rang. It was Rachel along with Ken and their friend Riley.

They'd brought some alcohol with them and we had a great night laughing and getting really drunk. As was often the case with me, the drunker I got the more confident I became and before too long I was behaving quite outrageously. Sober Emma, who could barely speak to a man, had disappeared and drunk Emma, who just wanted attention, was out and very loud. I don't know whether it was the alcohol, or what had happened with James, but I was feeling invincible and very provocative. I genuinely thought that the way I was acting around men was impressing them. The sad thing is that what I really wanted was respect and friendship, but I know now that I was never going to find it acting the way I did.

I found myself really flirting with Ken. He was twenty one, a lot younger than me, but I loved the attention. He was drunk and flirting back, and we started playing dares. The boys dared me to take my top off – which I did.

I woke up the next morning with a very poorly head and no memories of the night after taking my top off.

I saw Rachel later that day, she asked me if I could remember what I'd done. I said no, and she told me that Ken and I had had sex in front of her and Riley.

I was completely shocked, and absolutely mortified. I couldn't believe I could do something like that and have no memory of it!

When I ran into Ken the next day I was so embarrassed, I turned bright red. He told me that he'd had a really good night but that he wouldn't tell his cousin – who I was supposed to be seeing that weekend.

One of the worst things about being an alcoholic is trying to come to terms with the bad decisions you make when you're drunk. It's also one of the things that people can't see, and so often think that we don't care. I couldn't take away what I'd done; I couldn't erase or remove it, and once sober I had no coping mechanism either. I thought long and hard about whether to include some of the things I've done when drunk into this story because it's hard for me to come to terms with the fact that I've even done them, let alone admitting them to others. But part of coming to terms with who I am is coming to terms with what I've done and I can't do that if I'm still trying to pretend they didn't happen.

I feel sick with guilt as I write this. I wasn't some silly teenager who did a daft thing with no consequences. I was a mother and my children were in the house. Of course, what I should have been doing is letting my behaviour shock me into stopping drinking, but what it did was make me want to drink even more so that I could block out the memories and the truth of what I'd done.

In the end, drinking became a vicious circle. I'd get horrendously drunk and behave terribly, then I'd wake up sober with patchy or no memories of what I'd done. Someone would tell me or I'd begin to remember some parts of the previous nights and I'd want to drink just to deal with the guilt and disgust I had with myself.

Mark didn't turn up. Although he'd been texting me at the start of the week, the messages had tailed off by the end of the week and then stopped altogether. I was upset, but at the end of the day Mark was a young single man in the army and I was a woman with three children in the middle of a messy break-up. I never found out whether he knew about me and Ken, but I would guess so.

At the time, I had such a low opinion of men that I wasn't expecting anything different from him. I didn't believe that men could show commitment or faithfulness and I suppose that that's where a lot of my behaviour towards them came from. I reasoned that if men were allowed to have no-strings sex and flirting, then I could too, and damn anyone who didn't agree. It's a horribly flawed logic, but I was so broken by what James and I had done to each other, it was my way of protecting my heart from being hurt again.

The situation with James was horrible and we still weren't getting on, so when it came time for him to collect the children that weekend I decided I didn't want him at the house, and arranged to meet at the train station. We made small talk for the children's sake and I told him I was still seeing Mark. I was still hurting from not hearing from Mark and I certainly didn't want James to say, "I told you so."

I'd made plans to see Rachel again that night, and as James had taken the children, Rachel brought her friends again. I was really enjoying the partying by this stage, and I loved spending time with my new friends.

I met lots of new people that night, and although I couldn't remember a lot because I was so drunk, it was a great night. A few days later I ran into a girl called Tamsin, she had been to a party at my house that weekend. I had no memory of even meeting her, but she told me she'd had a good time and we actually had a good laugh about the fact that I couldn't remember her. By that point, my house was getting well known as a party house and I'd often have people I didn't know turning up. I never called any of these people my friends, but I thought at the time that they must have genuinely liked me otherwise they wouldn't have wanted to come round. I never even stopped to think that they were only using me.

I was starting to drink earlier in the day and was regularly used to not remembering large parts of the night. I also started to have parties during the week too. They were noisy and often woke the children up;

As far as I was aware, the people at my parties were nice to the children and as I'd put them to bed first, I honestly didn't think they'd be too disturbed by what was going on. It breaks my heart to find out when writing this that the parties, and the people who were coming to them were terrifying both Luke and Liam. Luckily, Ami was too young to remember anything about them but Luke told me that one person who came to the parties would get angry, was very loud and would smash bottles over his own head.

Sometimes the children would just make themselves scarce to avoid the parties and the people there. Luke would take himself, Liam and Ami to the beach or the park to get them out of the way. They'd come back and my "friends" would be hanging out of the window shouting at them to go away, that this wasn't their house any more. I would be in the background not noticing what was going on because I was so wrapped up in the parties and the drinking. It wasn't a case of me not caring because I genuinely did, however it might appear, but I was so far into my addiction that I just couldn't see the truth of the situation.

For a little while, Luke moved out. One night he came back from the beach and I refused to let him in. Our neighbours called the police and they took me to the station while they waited for someone to come and collect me. They rang Luke's Dad and he had to come down from Maidstone to collect him. Poor Luke waited for three hours to be collected and was terrified that they'd make him wait in a cell. After that he decided, rightly so, that he didn't want to live with me and ended up staying with James for a month.

When he came back, things were just as bad. We were falling apart as a family and as much as I'd wanted to show James that we could manage just fine without him, we needed him desperately; I just couldn't admit it.

There were some mornings when the hangovers were so bad that I couldn't even get out of bed, let alone take the children to school. Luke's attendance fell to only about 50%. He'd have to take days off because I wasn't capable of taking care of Liam and Ami. He's told me since, to my shame, that during those times he felt more like their father than their brother. He remembers that he had to make sure everyone ate properly, even though I'd never taught him how to cook and that for months we lived off microwave meals that he could manage making.

I should have been putting my children first and giving them a home they could feel safe in, but instead I turned their home into a nightclub with strange people coming and going. I can never give them back those days or take away the memories they must have and that sickens me.

Of the three of them, it was undoubtedly Luke who suffered the most: mainly because he was so aware of what was going on. I worry about how what happened back then has affected him in the long term and I feel utterly ashamed that I can never give him the kind of care-free childhood that I should have done. He spent a lot of time back then avoiding me, as anyone would have done. He'd get Liam and Ami ready for bed once they'd had their dinner and then go out, leaving me and my friends to it. Then he'd go to friends' houses to play video games. One of his closest friends had lived with us in the refuge and knew all about our situation so Luke had someone to talk to who understood what his life was like.

Beyond that, his life was awful and it was my fault. Because my illness came first, Luke, Liam and Ami never had the chance to experience a normal family life and it's little wonder that Luke has told me since that he used to hate coming home because he never knew what he was coming home to.

As well as our house having a reputation as party central, I was also getting myself a name; it was easy for guys to take advantage of "Drunk Emma" and I was sleeping around regularly. It's little wonder that people started to talk about me.

The partying was crippling us financially and with every spare penny I had going on alcohol, I was leaving myself and the kids short of money to live on. Ami was invited to a birthday party. With no money there was no way I could afford to buy a present for the birthday girl. I had a plan though! I went down to the local supermarket and stole a present for Ami to take.

I was surprised to find out just how easy it was to steal; I wasn't caught and I loved the thrill I got from getting away with it. After that, I decided I wanted a new top so the next time James took the kids I went into a clothes shop, walked into the changing room with the top I wanted and swapped it for an old vest top I was wearing underneath my clothes. I left the old vest on the hanger and walked out wearing my new top! Once again the feeling of getting away with it was thrilling!

Although I knew before that I was drinking too much, this was the first time that I can see I had a full blown addiction and that it had taken over my life. I had lost myself to such a degree that I was just living for the nights when I would drink. I put that above everything else and, financially, it became my priority. My clothes had become tatty, but I didn't care, I certainly didn't want to waste my precious money on replacing them because that would mean I'd have to cut into my drinking fund.

That evening I was expecting my usual houseful. Over the last few weeks, I'd met loads of new people. I became friends with a man called Dave. He was twenty four and had a terrible reputation. He'd been in and out of prison, but he was good to me and looked out for the kids.

I'd been arrested several times and I was still convinced that I was a good person underneath it all, so I decided to give Dave the benefit of the doubt. Like me, he had no family that he was in contact with and, despite the stories that followed him around, I trusted him. He was friends with two other blokes called Terry and Jermaine and the three of them usually turned up together.

It was late and nobody had arrived yet. I was just getting ready to go to bed, when there was a knock on the door. It was Dave with Terry and Jermaine along with Ken and Riley; they were all ready to party. I'd finished all of the alcohol I had in the house and, although I was drunk, I wanted more. But at eleven pm there was nowhere open locally.

I had no money either except my rent. I was dipping into the money regularly, but I told myself that a little more wouldn't hurt. Jermaine called a taxi and we went to the local supermarket to get another bottle of vodka. Luke and Liam were now awake as our party was keeping them up, so while Jermaine and I went out, Terry and Dave stayed with the children. Dave had always made a special effort to be nice to my three children and I knew they'd be okay with him and Terry for the short while we were out.

When we got back, I put the children to bed and told them they had to stay there as we were going to have some more drinks.

We started to down shots of vodka on top of what I'd already drunk and because I was still going for days without eating I was soon absolutely paralytic. I honestly don't remember what happened next but I woke up on the sofa the following morning surrounded by empty bottles and feeling dreadful, but thankfully fully clothed.

I ran to the toilet to be sick, then headed back to bed to recover and tried to piece together what had happened. I had a text message from Ken on my phone saying, "Had a wicked time last night. Was crazy, you were so funny."

I still couldn't remember a thing but had a feeling of dread. I can remember thinking, "Oh God, what did I do this time?"

I rang Ken to ask what I'd done and he told me that him and all the boys had urinated into a bottle and dared me to drink it. Not only had I drunk it but they filmed me too! I didn't believe him and thought it was a wind up. I thought there was no way I could have done that.

Tamsin rang later to see how I was and told me, to my utter horror, that Ken was telling the truth. The video was being shared around the local area. As far as I was told, they had started out as video messages on people's phones but had then been uploaded onto the internet.

I was devastated. I felt sick and used as well as totally betrayed. I'd done some things when I was drunk that I wasn't proud of, and I knew that I had a reputation, but I even frightened myself at what I was capable of. I felt completely sickened, not only by what I'd done, but also by the fact that I thought they were my friends and I'd allowed them into my home.

The terrifying part is that I had absolutely no memory of what I'd done.

Chapter 14

I felt dreadful and as the days went on, I found out more and more people had seen the video. I certainly found out who my friends were. Vicky, Rachel and Tamsin were brilliant, but other people decided I was a slut and hated me. I couldn't blame them really. Had I heard about another girl acting the way I did I would have felt disgusted too. I would have been judgemental, and it wouldn't have occurred to me that she was ill. As it was, I was disgusted with myself. I'd put myself into that position and I never regained the memory of it even happening.

I promised myself that I'd never let the boys in again. It was clear that, with the exception of Dave, they'd just wanted to take advantage of me. Nothing ever happened between Dave and I, and he showed himself to be a friend I could count on later. He obviously thought a lot of the children and on days where I was too hung-over to leave the house, he would collect Liam from playschool for me.

The whole time he was helping me, I knew that he had his own issues to deal with. I never got involved in his private life. I think that he was grateful for simply having somewhere to escape to.

As well as Dave, I still had support from the girls. Tamsin came around most evenings to make sure I was okay and keep me company. In addition I saw a lot of Vicky during the day and the weekends. She'd bring Clara round to play with Ami and we all became really close.

Although I was trying to hold it together, I was now drinking over a litre of vodka a day. I'd buy the cheapest brand I could find and because I was looking for strength, rather than taste or quality, it wouldn't matter. As well as spending every spare penny I had on alcohol, I also found a local shop which offered a tab service, so if things were tight that week I could still find a bottle.

As the backlash against me died down, James and I started talking again and we decided that as Luke's birthday was getting close, we should put all of our differences to one side and spend the day together as a family.

When James first came in, he didn't take off his sunglasses, he told me it was still very painful for him and he was worried about crying in front of the children and ruining our precious time together.

Throughout the day, I tried to explain to James that I didn't want him to try to control me. I liked having a drink, and I didn't need James trying to act like the parent in our relationship. He had to accept what I wanted to do. In return, James said that if I would let him come home, he wouldn't stop me from drinking.

I agreed and to seal the deal, we went to the shop together and bought a bottle of vodka. James ended up staying the night. After everything that happened, it should have been harder for me to let James come back, but deep down all I'd ever wanted was his love and acceptance of me.

I've thought a lot about why I needed James so much, I believe that a lot of it came from feeling vulnerable, insecure and all I wanted was to be loved.

I was stuck in a vicious circle: I was craving love and security, but once I had it I couldn't accept that it was real, so I'd feel the need to test or push it away. I was desperate to find a crack in anything good because that was all I'd ever known, and as a result every relationship, be it with a friend, lover or family, it turned into a mess.

It's only since coming into sobriety and working through all my issues that I can fully give love but believe I'm deserving of it too. One of the most important things about my recovery is the valuable relationships that have survived through this whole ordeal. I value those relationships more than ever now.

Despite going to bed with James happy, the following morning it hit me that I wasn't ready for James and I to be a couple again. As we'd already told the children, I felt I didn't really have a lot of choice and so a few days later, James moved back into the family home.

While we'd been apart, James had been working on a building site in Chelmsford, Essex. He'd been commuting every day from Maidstone so living with us again made his work much easier as we were closer to Chelmsford. On paper it was perfect, but I'd changed so much in the small time we were living apart that none of it seemed right.

Although some of my friends stayed away or kept their distance once James moved back in, we were still seeing a lot of Tamsin and luckily she and James got on. I was still struggling to cope with all the changes and missed having my own space; I was desperately craving some time by myself.

I didn't have to wait too long. While we'd been apart, James had booked a holiday to Devon with his family and the children. He wrestled with the idea of going at first, especially as I wasn't invited but I assured him it was ok.

His parents and other family members were dead set against us being together and moving back in with me had caused a lot of arguments once again. If I was watching someone treating any of my children as badly as I treated James, I know I'd feel exactly the same.

So it was agreed that I would stay at home whilst James went on the family holiday. I should have been worried or upset, but the truth was I felt I'd had little choice in letting him move back in and, in reality; we shouldn't have been in such a rush.

I had only allowed James to move back in because of the children, and whilst I was determined that they were my priority, I went about showing this completely the wrong way. I had no idea that I was disrupting them as badly as I was, and I had no concept of how much they were seeing that they should have been shielded from.

While James and the children were away, I was looking forward to some time to get my head together a little. James was concerned about leaving me but I persuaded him that some alone time would do me good.

Of course, by this time my reputation was well known and James had heard all about what I'd been up to. I promised him that I'd be on my best behaviour and would stay faithful, but by now my promises meant nothing, especially once I'd had a drink.

My plan whilst I was free of him and the children was to see my friends and party like I used to. Having no children meant I had no need to get up, so I drank even more than usual.

The girls came over one night with Dave and a guy called Pete, although Pete had arrived with Dave and they knew each other, it was apparent they weren't really friends.

As much as I was happy to see my friends, I was uneasy over Pete. He had a scariness about him and I didn't trust him, but he took a big shine to me and spent the night telling me that he could change my life. The whole time he was talking himself up, I was trying to snuggle into Dave. I had no interest in Dave in that way but I thought if Pete thought he had no chance with me then he'd leave me alone or just leave.

I'm sure that the only reason he was interested was because of my reputation for sleeping around.

While Pete made me feel unsafe, there was something comforting about Dave. He wasn't perfect at all and was often in trouble with the Police for being drunk or violent, but there was something about him that I trusted. He felt like a kindred spirit. He was reckless but I could see that it was just a cry for help. I often felt, especially in those days that with no family around there were no consequences to anything I did because there was nobody to care. Dave seemed to be the same and so I understood him.

With James away I had a lot of time to think about our relationship. I decided to tell James that living together didn't feel right: it was all just too much too soon. I knew that I'd only agreed to have him back to live with us because I felt sorry for him and, although I loved him and always would, I just wasn't in love with him anymore.

It was like a toxic rollercoaster. As soon as he returned from the holiday I told him and of course, he took the news badly. I felt terrible but I couldn't live a lie. He packed his stuff once again and moved out. Not surprisingly he hated me for what I'd done. History just kept on repeating itself.

Without James around to keep my behaviour in a relatively reasonable order, I started to drink heavily again. Although we'd agreed that he wouldn't control me, having James living with us again put us back into a routine of sorts. I think that everyone acts differently when they've got someone else living with them, whether it's putting make up on every day or doing the dishes before bedtime. James and I were no different and we simply fell back into the same routine we'd always been in while he was with me, but as soon as he'd gone I fell back into my routine as a single woman who wanted to party. At the time, I called myself a "free-spirit" and saw James as the person who wanted to anchor me and turn me into something I wasn't.

I thought I was having "real" fun, but in reality asking James to leave was quite possibly the most dangerous thing I could have done.

Some nights I would see my friends and we'd drink together, other nights I'd just drink alone. I was getting so drunk some nights that I couldn't even make my way to bed and would wake up on the sofa with an empty bottle.

The children were missing a lot of school and not surprisingly the school asked Social Services to get involved. Even that didn't force me to change my ways, instead I decided the whole world was against me and felt sorry for myself.

Without James to look after us, and me in no fit state most of the time, Luke became the man of the house. Without Luke we couldn't and wouldn't have coped, and yet to this day he's never rebelled. He had every right to and nobody would have been surprised if he'd gone off the rails, but he's always behaved and worked hard at school. I look at him now and feel a burst of pride for the young man that he's become. He carried far too much of the burden of looking after our family where I couldn't, how he survived I really don't know.

As a child himself he'd take care of us all. On school nights, he'd always set an alarm and make sure everyone was up on time. He'd get himself dressed and help with Liam and Ami and then take himself to school.

There were days when I couldn't leave the house because I felt so ill and on those days I'd beg Luke to either take the day off school to look after Liam and Ami or to be late so he could take them to school. Quite rightly he'd always say no to me.

Instead, he'd leave us alone and I'd sleep on the sofa while the children played. It must have been so boring for them staying in all day but I'd never hear a sound from them.

At the end of school, Luke would come home and make sure everyone had something to eat before helping me to get Liam and Ami into bed. Then he'd get on with his homework while I drank.

I was getting really aggressive when I'd had a drink, and it started to impact on my friendships.

After a night at my house with the girls I found a torn picture of Rachel in the fireplace. I couldn't remember anything from the night before but when I went to make a coffee I was horrified to see in the mirror that I had a black eye.

I checked my phone for clues and found lots of nasty messages from Rachel. I frantically tried to call her, but she kept rejecting my calls and wouldn't respond to the messages. After a while, Rachel's sister Lauren phoned me. She was very angry and asked me what the hell I was playing at. I didn't know why she was angry but she soon told me. Apparently I had been horrible to Rachel; I'd said some awful things to her and then tried to attack her – my black eye was from Rachel who was trying to defend herself from me flying at her.

I was horrified and begged Lauren to speak to Rachel for me. She said that she'd try and a little later Rachel rang to talk. She accepted my apology but it didn't make me feel any better. I'd now hurt one of my best friends and it was all because of alcohol. I felt so down.

Things would get worse that week when I received a letter from James' solicitor containing divorce papers. Although I'd ended things and pushed for a final separation, I couldn't believe it had turned out this way.

When we'd first got married, I'd been so sure about us and I so desperately wanted to make it work, even if it hadn't seemed like that in the end. The truth was that I never expected James to take that final step. He'd always looked after me, and I'd become used to the idea that he always would even if we weren't together. I didn't need him all the time but I wasn't ready for him to be gone forever either, and although it must sound cold I liked the idea of being able to go to him when I needed that extra support.

I never doubted that he loved me, or that he'd always be there for the children, but the finality of the divorce papers shocked me, and it did make me question how I really felt and if I'd acted too hastily in asking him to leave again. Once again I was confused as to my feelings for him. I was scared of losing him altogether but I didn't want him either.

Still, I stood and stared at the divorce papers and remember feeling that they were just one more thing I'd failed at. I read through them in floods of tears and then put them in a drawer thinking that if they were out of sight, then I wouldn't need to think about them.

I couldn't believe what a mess I was making of my life. I didn't know what I was expecting from life at the time and I didn't know what I wanted either, but I knew that everything felt like it was spiralling out of control and that was terrifying.

The next night I invited the girls round for a drink, I woke the following morning as usual with no recollection of what I'd done. But with a group of horrible text messages from Tamsin's brother, Mike telling me I'd called Tamsin fat! I couldn't believe it, I knew she was sensitive about her weight and I used this against her, this time I'd gone too far. I was horrified and tried desperately to get in touch with her, but she wouldn't take my calls and a little later Mike and our friend Ken banged on my door. They were horrible to me and told me that I was to never go near Tamsin again.

I felt so utterly heartbroken at being so cruel to one of my closest friends. She hadn't deserved it and out of everyone she'd always been loyal to me and there for the children. She'd been nothing but a good friend. The last thing I should have done was turn on her.

I closed the door, and shut all the curtains then poured myself a large drink. I felt awful – what had I turned into? I was a monster and I didn't deserve my friends, yet I still turned to the bottle for support.

Luckily, the children were spending the weekend with James so they'd missed what happened. I was grateful to be alone with my misery but then Pete called round. I didn't want him or anyone else there and tried to tell him that I wasn't in the mood for company. He didn't get the hint and followed me into the house then poured us both a drink. Just as he had on previous occasions he tried it on with me but rather than being flattered or amused as I had been before I found that I was just angry with him. Why wouldn't he get the message that I didn't want him? I made an excuse and went for a walk.

I needed time to think and decided to go and sit at the duck pond. I bought a bottle of vodka on the way and sat, in the pitch black, enjoying the silence.

I woke up with a start at three am and realised I'd fallen asleep by the pond. I was still drunk and although I remember feeling invincible from the vodka, my legs felt heavy and numb. It took me a long time to walk home as I was stumbling and falling all the way. To be honest I'm not sure how I managed to find my way home.

Still drunk but very cold, I stumbled home to find Pete still there waiting for me. I made another excuse and went to bed. I woke up the following morning, surprisingly with a clear head and found Pete still asleep. I snuck past him, grabbed my bank card and headed into town.

I finally knew what I wanted to do. I was terrified by who I was when I'd had a drink, but I couldn't let go of the bottle so this seemed like the only thing I had left. My life was a mess and I felt that everyone, including the children, would be better off without me around. For the first time in weeks I felt calm. I was certain that if I could end the pain I caused everywhere I went then it would be the best thing for everyone. I was terrified by who I was when I had a drink, but I couldn't let go of the bottle so this seemed like the only thing I had left.

I booked myself into a Bed and Breakfast. I didn't want the children to find me or have any bad memories; I had to go somewhere away from home. The following day was Easter Sunday, so I checked into the room then went to buy some Easter Eggs for them. I picked up as many boxes of Paracetamol and ibuprofen and as much alcohol as I could and went back to the Bed and Breakfast.

When I returned to the room I took about sixty tablets, washing them down with the vodka I'd bought. In the end I struggled to even swallow them, but I kept on going until I felt tired. I curled up on the bed and hoped it would all be over quickly.

I woke up about eight hours later feeling incredibly sick, it was just before midnight and I ran to the bathroom and started to vomit pure blood. I went back into my room and started to hallucinate. The dizziness from the drink and tablets was convincing me that the walls were moving and I could see things crawling up and down them. I was terrified. I realised that I was going to die here, in this very room; on my own. It's what I wanted hours ago, but this isn't how I wanted it to all end now.

I stood up again and tried to keep moving, trying to reach the bathroom, finding my reflection in the mirror, I cried out to myself to get help. I was a hopeless mess.

As I struggled around the room I was working myself into a terrible state. I kept remembering things James had said or done and I'd become hysterical. Then I'd think of the children and how much I'd hurt and damaged them. I'd remind myself of all of the horrible things I'd done to the ones I love so much.

I hated myself and who I was, but I was so scared that I had taken all those tablets and the thought of never telling them I was sorry frightened me. I didn't want this to be how they remembered me; I staggered out into the street in an attempt to get some help.

The next thing I knew I was waking up in a hospital bed.

Chapter 15

I was confused and disorientated for a few days and the effects of the tablets meant that I wasn't able to walk on my own or even speak. Initially I was treated as an emergency case, the following day they moved me from the high dependency unit to a normal ward.

I started to come round and understand more once I'd been moved to the ward, and it definitely helped that I was allowed to have visitors. I wasn't expecting to see anyone so I was so relieved when James turned up to see me. He threw his arms around me and I felt safe, breathing in the familiar smell of his leather jacket and crying. I couldn't believe he was still there for me, after everything I'd put him through. I knew I didn't deserve him and felt so lucky that he still cared.

I'd seen many doctors throughout my stay yet nobody had properly explained to me what was happening. Eventually I was told that it was the safest and best idea if I was transferred into a hospital which specialised in suicidal feelings and mental health problems. I was depressed and wasn't functioning properly, and they thought I would benefit from the specialist help they could offer me.

They went on to explain that I could agree to go voluntarily, but if I refused then they would have to section me under the Mental Health Act. I was scared.

James intervened and said that he wanted to help me get better. He asked the doctor if I could be moved to a unit closer to his home in Maidstone where he could give me the support I needed. I couldn't believe James still wanted to be a part of my life, my life felt like it was worth living if he was part of it.

The doctors agreed to James' plan and I was moved to the new unit a few days later. The whole situation was horrible and I felt completely out of it. My depression coupled with the medication I was on meant that I felt drained all the time. Even short conversations exhausted me and it got to the point that I could only get out of bed to eat and smoke.

The Mental Health Hospital felt like a place of limbo, it was as if I was floating somewhere between living and dying. I didn't want to live anymore, but I felt trapped as though I was being forced to stay alive, my emotions were all over the place and life felt strange and scary. The first hospital was busy with lots of nurses and care staff constantly checking up on me, but this felt much different. There wasn't as many staff and the only company was a group of people who were just like me – we had to find our own way of making it through the day and hope for the best. It got to the point that the only thing I had to look forward to was the nightly medication run – where a cup of pills could knock me out and I could escape my thoughts.

Once I'd settled into the unit, I started to see different doctors and counsellors. The hospital's policy was for us to see a doctor every three days for an assessment and evaluation, and over that time they tried a variety of medications to try and lift my mood. With each different pill I'd hope to feel different or better, but nothing seemed to do the trick.

Being in the hospital felt a lot like being in a zoo. There were doctors with clipboards continually watching us, and then writing notes and doing assessments. They would discuss what they'd observed during my private session later.

I was given a room with another person, but for the first time in a long time I didn't want to socialise. The room had a divider for our own privacy and I kept it closed all the time, even though the nurses tried to get me to open it. There were communal areas and lounges, but I stayed in my own room trying to come to terms with what had happened. Everyone I saw had the same vacant or traumatised expression on their face; the same expression I saw every time I looked in the mirror. It haunted me.

After a long counselling session, I was called in to chat with one of the doctors. He explained that he wanted to talk about my life, and asked lots of questions about myself. There were so many, that I simply can't remember all of them but those that stuck out were about my relationships. The doctor wanted to know if I had been promiscuous or put myself in situations which were dangerous or had a high risk. He also asked how I was looking after myself. Was I eating properly and paying attention to personal hygiene? Then there were questions about my spending; did I spend money frivolously or carelessly and wind up leaving myself nothing to pay bills with. Finally, he asked about my moods. Did I find myself veering dramatically from being happy to depressed and suicidal?

He kept reminding me to be completely honest, saying that if I wanted to feel better then I needed to be truthful with my answers. He was very reassuring.

I felt as though he'd looked inside my head and knew the truth about me. I could relate to everything he was saying and asking, so I decided to be absolutely honest. I relaxed for the first time and told him about the last few years of my life. I told him about stealing from shops and the other things I would do for excitement. I told him that I'd slept around and how I'd used alcohol to cope. For the first time I was honest about my varying moods and the amount I was drinking.

As I was talking to the doctor, I was watching him intently. I could see him scribbling notes and nodding as though what I was saying was making perfect sense. I suddenly realised the enormity of it all and felt I couldn't breathe, I started to really cry. If what I was saying and describing were symptoms of something then there might be a reason I acted the way I did, and the relief of that was almost too much to cope with.

Finally, after what seemed like a lifetime of questions, he sat back and started to talk. It took a long time to get to the diagnosis, then he explained that everything I'd said and described sounded like I was suffering from Bipolar Disorder.

I'd heard a little about Bipolar Disorder before, but nobody I knew had it. It was more of a celebrity illness in my opinion and it took a while for it to sink in that it wasn't just famous people who had it – I did too. James had been certain that I had some mental health problems and had urged me to get help for as long as I could remember. Now it looked like he had been able to see what the doctor was seeing and finally I was in the right place, getting all the help I desperately needed.

The doctor went into detail to explain about Bipolar Disorder and why it was making me act the way I did. Up until recently, it was called Manic Depression and it affects about one in every hundred adults at some point in their life.

A person suffering from Bipolar will have cycles of mood swings lasting for weeks or even months. During that time, their behaviour will be erratic and severe with extreme highs to extreme lows.

He went on to explain that there are three types of Bipolar and I was suffering from mild manic episodes called "Hypo-Mania." The symptoms for this type of Bipolar were behaving erratically, reckless spending, being overly familiar or critical of other people, having a very high sex drive and making spur of the moment choices with devastating consequences.

Just like they had with me, many people with Hypo-Mania find that their relationships with friends and family are strained by their behaviour, especially as many people do not understand our actions.

This sounded huge and terrifying to me, but the doctor explained that I would be started on some new medication immediately and that these had a good chance of changing the way I was feeling. He was very firm as he described my treatment process and told me, categorically, that I would have to stop drinking in order for the tablets to work properly.

When James came to visit me that evening I told him what had been discussed, I expected him to be shocked, but he just looked relieved. Of course, he'd known for a long time that things weren't right.

With James' support, I started the new treatment and to my joy the next few weeks were so much better. I started to feel better about myself and the tablets started to improve my moods. Along with James, Alison was the only person who came to visit me in the hospital. Despite all of the problems that we'd had, I really started to look forward to James' visits. I realised how much I'd missed him and the support he gave me. Everything that I'd found in the meantime with my so-called friends had been empty or one sided but what I had with James was genuine unconditional love and support and I began to see just how lucky I was to have him around. Over the weeks, those feelings began to develop further and it was like falling in love all over again.

As well as wanting to see James, I missed the children and grew desperate to see them.

I'm sure people who are lucky enough to have never suffered

from depression, or any other mental illness, will find it difficult to understand why I would have wanted to take my own life, especially when I say how much I love my children. The night I took the overdose, I wasn't thinking about anyone else. Not because I didn't care about them, or because I was trying to be selfish, but because I just wanted the pain to stop. I was destroying everyone around me and I thought they would all be better off if I wasn't around anymore.

Feeling this way is never deliberately selfish, it's simply part of the condition and it's very easy for me to understand how someone can want to take that final step to freeing themselves of their pain.

I think that one of the hardest things about depression is that there are no physical symptoms and so to someone looking from the outside in, it must seem that everything is okay. The person doesn't limp or have a rash so they can't possibly be "ill." In some ways that's the worst part, because trying to describe what's going on beneath the surface is nearly impossible.

While I was in hospital, James had been given custody of the children and they had found us a house to live together in Maidstone. James told me that the children were missing me and wanted to see me too. Then he asked the question I had been praying for – would I leave my life in Southend and come to Maidstone to reunite our family?

The doctors had told him that I was ready to leave and he wanted to look after me and our children. As delighted as I was, I was also terrified; I had upset and offended so many people in Maidstone. The thought of going back there was frightening, but my life in Southend was also in tatters. When I thought about my home back there, I felt sick with the shame that once again, I had managed to destroy the new life I'd had such high hopes for.

While I was in hospital, I had lots of counselling sessions and although some of them were just me and the doctor or therapist, others involved James. One in particular stuck in my head because it was the first time I'd ever seriously addressed the problem of my drinking in front of him.

I remember sitting in a room with James holding my hand while the doctor and the counsellor discussed the treatments I'd need when I left the hospital. She looked me straight in the eye and said "Emma, you really have to realise that you have a big problem here. You are an alcoholic and you must admit this now." She was kind but very straightforward in the way she was talking to me and, for the first time, someone had my attention when they were discussing how much I drank.

I started to cry and she took my hand, "From now on, every time you look at a bottle of alcohol, you must start to see it as a poison you're putting into your body, a poison you are putting into your family and your children's lives."

As she was saying the words, I was replaying all of those moments from the last few years when I'd hurt, felt pain or caused pain, I broke down as she spoke those harsh truths. I finally admitted out loud that I was an alcoholic and agreed that I couldn't cope any more. For the first time, I confessed that I both needed and wanted help.

The doctor then took over to explain about the physical damage the alcohol was doing to my body. As well as alienating my friends and family, I was hurting myself by drinking as much as I was and after a while my body would be unable to recover. My liver and other organs would stop functioning. In short, I was putting myself at a huge risk by carrying on drinking.

I felt terrified, and told them honestly how hard it was for me to say no to a drink. I told them that I'd tried to stop or cut down before, but I'd found it so hard, I just couldn't do it.

And for the first time, I wasn't alone. The doctor and the counsellor started to tell me about all of the avenues I had available for help. I could go to Alcoholics Anonymous meetings as well as local charities such as the Kenward Trust.

I left the room promising them, and James, that I would get the help I needed.

I went back to my room and thought about my options. I knew that all I wanted was to be with James and the children. I promised James and the doctors that I would attend Alcoholics Anonymous meetings, and in return the doctors told me that for the first few weeks a carer from the access team would see me every day to check on my progress.

After a month in hospital, the day came for me to finally go to our new home. I was scared but hopeful and, above all, I couldn't wait to see the children. I knew that things between me and James were massively different too. He looked worn out with the strain of the last few weeks. I realised that I'd done that to him, he was exhausted because of my addiction and my actions. I realised how lucky I was to have this wonderful man who was moving heaven and Earth to not only mend our relationship and family, but also help me to get better again.

Once we'd arrived home, I heard him taking phone calls from his family who were devastated that he'd let me come home. I heard him time after time defending me, our relationship, and our family. Watching him standing up for me, after everything I'd done to him, made me melt completely and I fell in love with him all over again. This man really loved me and I couldn't believe just how much. I started to see that this full and happy home was what I'd wanted all my life, not the partying with random strangers. I knew that I had to find a way of showing James just how much he meant to me.

The whole time I was in hospital, I hadn't been able to have a drink and being sober had given me the chance to have a long look at myself. For the first time in a long time I was finally seeing things clearly, and I knew that I didn't have any choice but to make this work.

Now I was back at home, I knew I had to make up for lost time with the children. I'd put them through an awful ordeal and we needed to rebuild our family. It took them a while to realise that I was different than the Mummy they'd been seeing for the last few years, but once they saw a difference in me, I was shocked by the difference in them. They were happier and the entire house just seemed calmer. We spent quality time together in the day by going to the park and taking picnics with us. The night times were calmer too; there'd be no more screaming at bedtimes. The whole house seemed a peaceful place and our family became more settled.

The children told me all the time how lovely it was to have Mummy and Daddy back together again, and I told them how much I loved them. I knew in my heart that I should have been making them my priority from the very beginning, I just hadn't realised my addiction was an illness. I now had to show them that they were the centre of my world.

Being with my family only strengthened my willpower and I was determined that I would keep all the promises I'd made. The only promise I didn't keep was to go to Alcoholics Anonymous meetings. I felt so strong at home with my family that I didn't think I needed them. I talked to James all the time about how I was feeling and we both seemed so happy with the progress I was making, so we never pursued getting the extra help.

I settled well into our new home, but still didn't have the confidence to go into Maidstone town centre. I just didn't feel comfortable there, but thankfully our new house was far enough away that I didn't need to go into the town centre for anything.

That summer was sunny and hot, we made the most of it by going out as a family at the weekends. James would search online for a place for us to visit and we'd set off with a picnic. One day he found a castle; it wasn't a long drive, so we set off only to find a set of ruins. Another time we might have been disappointed, but we ended up having a lovely day. We were the only people there so, as the children played, James and I sat down by the stream. We lay there looking up at the clouds, holding each other for what felt like an eternity. We had a lot to talk about and finally we opened up about everything that had happened over the last few years. We both had lots of questions for each other. I knew that because of everything we'd been through we'd both changed, but I was starting to see just how much I needed James and how much we still loved each other.

I never realised until I lost him, that James was my best friend. He was my partner in everything and I had missed him more than I could have ever realised. As well as feeling so much love for him, I also knew that I had him to thank for my family. Without him or his unending faith in me I wouldn't have been there with my children.

I knew in those perfect moments that being the complete and happy family we were was the most important thing to me. While sober I realised just how much I was still in love with James, but it was different than the feelings I'd had when I was drinking. With my other friends, I'd felt used and taken advantage of whereas with James all I felt was genuine love and keeping that love became the only thing that mattered.

Chapter 16

On top of my blossoming relationship with James, I was still seeing the doctor and the mental health teams regularly, as well as having weekly counselling sessions. Between these and the tablets, I was finally feeling better; I was in control and felt balanced. Best of all, I felt like I finally appreciated what I had, rather than looking outside our family for people who didn't care about me.

As I started to feel stronger and better, James and I agreed that I would start to help out with the school runs. I was excited about spending time with the children on my own and after everything that had happened I'd realised all that they'd been missing when I'd been drinking, I wanted to prove to them I cared about what they did at school and everything else in their lives.

So, just for a few mornings to start with, I walked Luke to his school bus and then took Liam to school with Ami in her pushchair. It was a little nerve wracking at first, especially as all of the other parents seemed to know each other and I felt like an outsider, but slowly, people began to say hello.

The children started to get invites to parties and some of the mums invited me to join their coffee mornings and baby groups with Ami and it seemed we were becoming part of the community.

As much as I was enjoying the life we were building, I was starting to feel myself struggle. I've often described myself as having two personalities. Jekyll and Hyde or Drunk Emma and Sober Emma. I'd managed to keep Drunk Emma away for the past few months but as I started to spend more time alone, walking to and from school and during the day where the boys would be at school and Ami would be having a daytime nap, I started to feel Drunk Emma like a devil on my shoulder.

At first, I'd just fancy a drink. It was a fleeting feeling and as soon as it had started it was gone so it was easy to dismiss but once I'd felt that initial longing, the craving started to become more intense.

I'd find myself walking into the kitchen and fetching a glass down from the cupboard. I'd do it without a second thought, it was habit and I wouldn't even realise what I'd done until I was standing looking at an empty glass.

I'd feel annoyed with myself and for letting my other self begin to bubble to the surface once more.

When I left the hospital I promised myself that I'd find a support group like Alcoholics Anonymous or another locally run network. I genuinely thought I was doing well and so I hate to admit I didn't actually go and find the support I obviously needed at the time. I'd made promises to James and was determined I would keep them. As much as I accepted that I had a problem, I didn't want to have to talk about it and I certainly didn't feel up to sharing my problems with a group of strangers.

When I finally did attend those meetings several months later, I realised just how important it is to share; talking about the cravings and the need to have a drink helps the drinker to stay strong and resist. I felt that bottling my feelings was the answer to my problems, but I was about to find out that the Hyde part of my personality wasn't going to be as easy to deal with as I wanted her to be.

My cravings for alcohol grew stronger and stronger, and as much as I hated them and wished they'd leave me alone, my feelings towards drinking were starting to change.

The doctors and counsellors at the hospital had told me, along with James, that the only way to cure my addiction was complete sobriety. For the last few months I'd been living with that sobriety and as they said, it was perfect.

The problem was that I was starting to believe in my own strength a little too much. Soon, the devil on my shoulder wasn't just whispering to me to give in to the craving. She was telling me that if I was strong enough to stay sober for months at a time, I was strong enough to only drink a little at a time.

I started to believe what I was telling myself. I'd just have a small drink because one couldn't or wouldn't hurt, James would never need to know and I could carry on living a normal life.

For weeks, I resisted that nagging whisper. I knew I couldn't have a drink. I'd promised James and the children that I'd never drink again and I wouldn't let them down. We were on the cusp of building such a fantastic life and I wouldn't be the one to ruin it again.

The problem was that once I'd let the nagging in, it wouldn't stop and everywhere I looked were people enjoying drinking. We lived down the road from a pub and in the lovely summer afternoons, I'd see people sitting outside in the beer garden enjoying each other's company, laughing and relaxing in the sun.

I'd walk past and envy them for how relaxing having a drink in the afternoons was. Then I'd feel furious with myself for daring to think that way and by the time we arrived home, I'd have worked myself up into a terrible mood. James would ask why I was so cross and I'd resent him for forcing me into making the promises to never drink again.

Of course he'd done no such thing but by that point, I wasn't thinking clearly. I was simply thinking about just how much I wanted a drink.

At the same time, James was started to get back into his music. He'd already decided to go back to college to learn Sound Engineering which was something he'd always wanted to do and once a week he'd go to his friend Paul's for a jam.

The next time he went out, I decided that it wouldn't hurt if I had a small drink and so I walked over to the local shop. I didn't want to get drunk and as much as I'd missed having a drink I hadn't missed the hangovers so that night I just brought a miniature bottle. There was enough for one shot of vodka and I topped it up with plenty of coke. I was determined to show that I could have just one and be fine. I went home and made sure the children were okay and tucked up in bed and then I closed the kitchen door.

Alarm bells should have sounded, I was shaking with fear as I opened the bottle. I knew that I shouldn't be drinking but I told myself that it was just the one and that I wouldn't do it again, James would never need to find out.

As the heavily diluted vodka slipped down my throat, I began to get the familiar feeling; it was like my troubles were drifting away and I couldn't believe how much I'd missed the buzz and how relaxed I felt. Once I'd finished, I put the bottle in my bag to get rid of on the way home from school the following morning. I cleaned my teeth and went to bed, happy and calm.

Up until that night, I hadn't had any opportunity to have a drink. Between the hospital and being at home with James and the children was very much a case of out of sight out of mind. The problem was that once I'd broken that initial barrier, all the old feelings came flooding back and the weeks

I'd been working so hard to stay sober were now ruined.

I should have known, in hindsight, that I could never just have "one drink" or be like everyone else and drink in moderation with no consequences, but at the time I didn't have the strength to say no. I was an addict, and whatever lived inside me that made me different from James, my friends and family and anyone else, had woken up.

I've made a lot of wishes in the last few years, but one of my biggest is here. I wish that I'd never had that first drink. I wish I'd never compromised my family or broken my sobriety because at that moment in time it was the worst thing I could have done.

Of course, once I'd got the taste back, I missed it even more. So I rationalised with myself that I could have just the one when James went out. I even went as far as to tell myself that I was doing him a favour by not telling him because it would only make him worry.

I never set out to deceive him, as an addict, you get used to telling yourself what you want to hear and you tend to surround yourself with people who do the same.

But as much as I was enjoying my secret drinking, I started to resent James for not letting me drink in front of him. Of course, he had no idea I was drinking in secret and the resentment was all in my head. It didn't help that when James went over to his friend's house to jam with them, they'd have a beer. In my head, as I was trying to justify my own behaviour, I started to think it was horribly unfair that James got to do something I wanted but couldn't.

I didn't have anyone to talk about how I was feeling so I became lost in my thoughts. Within a very short space of time, I went from being able to handle just the one to desperately wanting more.

I started to think of the voice in my head as a separate person and somehow we decided together that I was going to confront James to tell him that I wanted to start drinking again. I'd managed to convince myself that James was just being a bully by not wanting me to drink and I firmly believed that he was just trying to control me.

I sat down with him one night and told him straight that I wanted to drink again. Not surprisingly he went mad! He said that there was no way I could do this and refused to speak to me for days. In the past I might have begged him or tried to compromise but this time I wouldn't budge. I stopped sleeping with him and refused to speak to him properly – in my head he had become my enemy and I intended to treat him accordingly.

We had days like that, peppered with rows and eventually after one particularly big row James stormed out. He slammed the door and was gone for hours. When he came back he had a bottle in his hand for me. He looked utterly devastated but I was so pleased to have "won," that I either didn't notice or didn't care. I took myself off to the kitchen to get some glasses and toasted my victory.

Quite possibly the biggest mistake of my life.

Chapter 17

Once James had brought that bottle home; I carried on drinking. It got to the stage where I was back on the vodka every night again and I didn't care how much it was bothering James. I'd been drinking in secret and had been fine. I'd still been up with the children every morning so in my head, I'd proved that I could handle what I was doing.

I felt invincible. I was telling myself everything I wanted to hear and could block everyone else out, saying they were just being boring or controlling. As an addict, I tended to hear what I wanted and anyone who said something negative or that I wasn't ready to face was simply dismissed as being against me or out to get me. I can see now how dangerous it was for me to think that I could drink like other people could but at the time I was just back to being "me" having fun. Of course, being back in that frame of mind meant that everything the doctors and counsellors had said went straight out the window.

I was still making sure I spent time with the children during the day and we'd go to the park, for a lovely walk around the lake and shopping to pass the time. Then, once the children had gone to bed, I'd start drinking. Over a relatively short period of time, I'd increased the amount I drank to get the effect I needed and before too long, I was back to a bottle of vodka a night.

I got back in touch with Alison and although it had been a few years since we'd last seen each other, we soon clicked back into place. We might have changed and we'd both been through a hell of a lot, but with each other we were still exactly the same; laughing the whole time and being silly.

Even though it was easy being with Alison, I still found I wanted a drink before I saw her. I felt shy and self-conscious without a drink and thought I was coming across as quiet and awkward but once I'd had a drink I was confident and sure that I was much better that way.

Before Alison came round I would have a sneaky drink. I'd normally buy three miniature bottles of vodka and hide them upstairs. Then I'd make excuses to sneak up to my room to down the shots.

Alison had never been a big drinker like I was, so I never mentioned it to her – and she never talked about it at the time. As I started to write this story, I asked Alison about her memories. I had been oblivious to anyone else at the time but now I wondered just how much she had seen.

Alison told me that although she'd never been aware I was drinking before she arrived, she had popped round in the afternoon a few times to find me sitting drunk in the garden. She knew at the time that it wasn't right, and that it was out of character even for me. Then she told me something that will stick with me forever. She said I always wanted a drink because it made me feel better – but it made everyone else feel worse.

She was right, and as I started to drink heavily again, James and I were starting to see problems. His mum and dad had decided to give me another chance and James was terrified that they'd find out I was drinking again. James just couldn't relax and was on edge the whole time. I was only too happy for them to be part of our lives as they loved the children and the children loved them too so I never drank in front of them and we never talked about it either but James was on edge and would nag me; especially when it became hard to hide my hangovers from them.

James would watch me like a hawk while I was drinking and seemed to be constantly keeping count of how much I'd had and how often.

Not surprisingly, things started to take a turn for the worse. In my head, James was quickly turning into the enemy again – the dull person who didn't want me to have fun and I found myself thinking that James just wanted to spoil things.

Our arguments were starting to get nasty again and one Sunday morning, I woke up alone with a terrible headache. James was nowhere to be seen, so I headed downstairs to find him. He'd slept on the sofa and when I woke him up, he was furious. He swore and shouted at me, for reasons I didn't know.

The noise quickly upset the children and they started to cry which only made me angry. I screamed back at him to tell me what was the matter, and in absolute fury he rolled up his sleeve and showed me his forearm. It was covered in marks and bruises but I still didn't know why.

Then James told me. The night before, I was sitting outside the back door having a cigarette. I'd had quite a lot to drink and James told me to come inside. I hadn't wanted to and we'd started arguing about how much I'd had to drink. One thing led to another and I'd stormed into the bathroom and locked myself in. I was standing inside, swearing and yelling at James who'd had no choice but to kick the door down.

Once he got into the bathroom, I attacked him. I flew at him trying to hit him and as he tried to restrain me, I had bitten down hard on his arm, refusing to let go.

The marks on his arm were bite marks from me.

I felt sick to my stomach but couldn't believe, or accept, what

I was seeing. I felt sure that he must be trying to wind me up, so I stormed down to the park to give myself a chance to cool off. I grabbed my coat and my packet of cigarettes on the way and sat shaking as I tried to come to terms with what James had told me.

I couldn't remember anything of what he'd said but I felt sure he must have been making it up or making it seem worse. Maybe if he'd just left me alone then nothing would have happened. After all, said the little voice in my head, we only argued when he tried to stop me from having fun.

After a while, I thought I'd better go home and I knew that I had a lot of making up to do. So I went home and begged for James' forgiveness. I really did feel that I wasn't to blame for everything but that didn't stop me from feeling horrible about what had happened. The marks on James' arm took weeks to heal, they looked just as red and angry as they had the morning after. It really looked like they were going to leave a permanent scar.

I was terrified that someone would see my bite marks and knew that I had a lot of making up to do. It was over a week before James would even begin to start speaking to me again and for a good few weeks after that, I was very careful about the amount I had to drink.

Things between myself and James slowly calmed down a little, and we were invited over to my friend Lucy's house for the night. I'd been to school with her and she and her husband Frank had been in touch with us a few times since we moved back to the area. Lucy had always been up for a laugh and I knew she liked a drink so I was looking forward to a good night out. We'd asked Jenny and Rich if they would look after the children and as the day of the party arrived, I got really excited.

I could tell James wasn't looking forward to it at all though, and who could blame him after past experiences. He said he didn't really want to go and was getting fed up of doing nothing except drinking all the time. He was getting really worried about what I was capable of doing when I was drunk.

I was so angry with him that I started a huge row. I told him I was going with or without him and eventually he reluctantly agreed that he would go.

I was delighted to have won our argument and poured myself a vodka to celebrate while I got ready. As much as I'd been looking forward to the party, when it actually got to the point that I had to put my clothes on ready to go, I started to feel sick with nerves. I always got nervous and felt that I was only confident once I'd had a drink so I downed a few more shots while I waited for James to finish getting ready.

I drank so much that afternoon that I don't remember finishing getting ready, let alone actually leaving the house but I woke up the following morning in bed alone.

Amazingly I didn't have a hangover but still felt as though I was drunk. I walked downstairs feeling completely confused and trying to work out what had happened and where James was. The last thing I remembered was drinking the shots for my "confidence" so maybe I hadn't even made it out of the house. I couldn't remember anything and I couldn't find any clues around the house.

I walked into the living room and found James sitting with his head in his hands. I braced myself for an argument or a tirade from James but he just looked at me with disgust then walked past me to go back to bed.

"Moody idiot" I thought to myself, and went out into the garden for my first cigarette of the day. I was standing in the garden when I had a sudden image pop into my head of James and I arguing. We weren't at home and I couldn't place where we were. I could hear laughter and loud music but felt terrified that I had no idea where or when this happened. My head started to pound and I knew I would have to go and face James to ask him what had gone on.

When I got to the top of the stairs, I could hear him moving about in bed so I put my head around the door. "James" I said, gingerly "What happened last night? I feel terrible and I can't remember anything."

He looked at me coldly, "which bit would you like first?" he snapped "The bit where we nearly got thrown out of a taxi? The bit where we got kicked out of a party? Or the bit where you screamed and shouted at Luke and I?"

I couldn't believe what I was hearing. I didn't remember a thing.

"What happened?" I told him, feeling sick with dread.

James explained. I'd been drinking for most of the afternoon when he told me I had to get ready or we would miss the party. I told James I needed to stop on the way to get more vodka. He'd known that if we didn't then I'd start an argument before we got anywhere so he'd planned to let me buy some and then water it down so much that I would sober up. We'd stopped at a supermarket to buy some vodka and while James was inside, I'd been rude to the taxi driver. When James got back to the car, the driver was standing outside refusing to drive us anywhere. James didn't know what I'd said but had to promise the driver that he'd keep me under control until we got to the party.

I couldn't believe what I was hearing, but by James' face and the tone of his voice, I knew things were about to get much worse. Finally we had arrived at Lucy's house and for some reason I got it into my head, and was absolutely convinced, that I was at a farm. I don't have a single memory of Lucy's house but I kept walking about asking people why I'd been brought to a farm.

Of course, everyone at the party thought it was hilarious and some of Lucy's friends started to laugh at me. I didn't like being laughed at and I went on the offensive, telling people to fuck off and apparently I'd tried to start several fights.

Lucy was of course really cross with me and wanted me to leave, especially as it looked as though some of her friends were ready to finish the fights I was desperate to start.

James called a taxi to take me home but by the time it arrived I was in an even worse state. I was sick on the pavement and then started to swear loudly at the poor driver. Not surprisingly the taxi driver refused to take us and drove away. Luckily, one of Lucy's friends agreed to take us all home.

How could I have done all that and not remember a thing? My legs started to wobble and I could feel my face getting hotter and hotter as though I was going to be sick. Then a craving for a drink hit me and I felt so woozy I thought I would need to sit down.

I tried to reach out to James to say sorry but he hadn't finished yet.

After we got home, I had started to scream and shout at James for not letting me stay, saying that I could have handled Lucy's friends. Luke had come into the room to try and calm us down and I'd turned on him too.

Not surprisingly, Luke was furious with me and had every right to be. From what James was telling me, they both had every right to hate me for what I'd done to them again.

I stared at the floor in silence, willing myself not to vomit and wishing I could just turn back time. When I finally found the courage to look James in the eye, I started to really cry. I didn't want any arguments. I just wanted to say I was sorry, and for him and Luke to believe me.

James hugged me and let me cry. All the time, he was telling me and begging me to calm down and not drink as much. I agreed and promised him I would, but the whole time I knew that there was no way I could go without a drink that night!

And so I had another reminder that I really shouldn't be drinking. I felt terrified all the time and it felt as though the alcohol was a crutch that I needed just to get through the day – yet it was the biggest problem I had and the biggest cause of the troubles I was going through.

The thought of being able to go on an entire night out and not remember a thing was just awful. Then hearing about all the things I'd done while not being able to recall a single memory just made me feel ashamed of myself.

Yet, all the while I'm hearing this awful story of what I'd done, I was desperately in need of drink to calm my nerves. I was using those feelings to justify having a drink later that night. If I could just blot out those feelings then I could find a way to feel better, or simply forget they existed. The fact that the drinking had caused those feelings in the first place wasn't something I was ready to face.

I was truly, and undeniably addicted.

Chapter 18

Despite my promises earlier that night I carried on drinking and as much as James had been angry with me at first, his anger just turned into sadness and disappointment with me.

Things just seemed to be getting worse and worse for us – and it was all to do with the amount I was drinking. When James and I got back together after my release from hospital, we felt like we were starting again. I had fallen in love with him all over again and we were Team Bushen. We took our courage from each other and it was only when I returned to drinking that the strength we'd found together showed signs of weakening.

We received some sad news just a few weeks later. The lady who ran our local shop had passed away. She'd become a friend to all of us, and was well regarded in the community. She was a lovely woman who always had a smile and a lollipop for the children and it was obvious that she'd be missed by everyone.

The shop was part of a big chain so the company who owned it sent a new manager and I soon got to know Gloria. She moved into the flat above the shop with her family.

As I was a of course a regular customer, I quickly got to know her and started to have a laugh when we went in, especially as I was often a little merry and in to purchase my bottle each day.

I started to see her all the time. Her grandchildren went to the same school as Liam and Ami so I'd see her at the gates and if we went into town or the park she always seemed to be around. I suppose it's like that in any community. Although we used to have a laugh together there was something about her that I couldn't quite take to.

The first time I noticed that there might be a problem was one morning a few weeks after she'd moved in. James and I had had another row and I'd flounced off to the shop to buy a bottle of vodka.

When I got to the shop, there was a woman I knew from the school gates standing in the queue. Ami had had an invitation to her little girl's birthday party and so I caught her eye and said "Ami's looking forward to the party." The woman smiled and was just about to say something when Gloria fixed me with a filthy look and said "Excuse me. We're in the middle of a private conversation here. Are you always this rude?"

I couldn't believe it and must have looked very shocked. The poor woman didn't know what to do either and must have seen that I was close to tears, especially as the argument with James was so fresh in my mind, so she smiled nervously. Gloria started laughing and said "Oh, don't mind me. You know I always say what I think," brushing off what she'd said and the way she'd said it.

I didn't really know what to do but didn't want to start an argument with someone we saw on such a regular basis so I laughed too but felt upset.

When I got outside the woman was waiting for me around the corner. "Wow" she said "Are you okay? That seemed really out of order." I was glad that it wasn't just me but didn't want to start criticising Gloria to someone I hardly knew so I just smiled and said

"Oh yes, she's always like that. I don't think she means anything by it."

I wasn't sure of that at all. For some reason, Gloria had taken against me and I had no idea why.

A few days later, Ami and Liam asked if they could go and play with their friends next door. I looked through the window and saw two other children with them. I called out to my neighbour to ask if it was ok for Ami and Liam to come and play as they often did. She said of course and introduced my two to Gloria's grandchildren.

I told her to shout if six kids in her garden got too much for her. Then I went back inside to carry on with my jobs. I kept the door open so that I could hear what mine were up to and shortly after I heard Gloria's voice.

"Hello poppets" she laughed and then the tone of her voice changed "oh, and you two. Well I haven't got anything for you." She said the last bit coldly so I went straight outside to see what was going on.

"Hiya" she said "I brought ice lollies for the four children. I didn't realise yours were here too so they haven't got anything."

"That's okay," I smiled as nicely as I could manage "I've got some inside for mine." I turned around, planning to get two lollies out of my freezer and heard that she'd muttered something under her breath. I didn't catch it but knew it wasn't very nice.

It wasn't the only time that I didn't like the way she treated me or my children. One time Liam said hello to her grandson on the way home from school and she scowled at him. Another, I saw her pass a sweet nicely to her two grandchildren and another two children and then practically throw one at Ami. It caught Ami by surprise, and she let out a little cry. Gloria knew that I'd seen what she'd done and she made a huge fuss about giving Ami a hug and saying that she was sorry, all the while mouthing "she's so sweet" in such a fake manner to me.

Although I had no proof other than a bad feeling, there was something about Gloria that really unnerved me. Then, a few weeks later I had an email from an old friend from School. She'd seen me add Gloria as a contact on a social media site.

I'd only added her because Gloria had sent me a friend request, but Jade told me to be on my guard. She knew Gloria from her old job and told me that Gloria had bullied her to the point that Jade almost had a breakdown. She gave me a few examples of what happened and based on what I'd seen I had no trouble believing her. Then finally she warned me to be very careful around her.

I quickly typed a message back thanking Jade and telling her that I was already on my guard. The silly thing was that I'd only added her as a friend because I didn't want to be rude when she ran the local shop and a lot of the other locals had added her as a contact. I thought it might seem childish not to.

I was in a terrible state after getting the email and decided to have a drink to calm my nerves while I waited for James to come home. I wanted to tell him as soon as possible what had happened and what Jade had said in her email. I didn't just stop at one drink though and by the time James arrived, I was so drunk that I wasn't in any fit state to talk to him. Instead we just ended up having another furious row!

A few weeks later, Liam was standing in our front garden saying hello to people as they passed by. He often did it and loved having a chat with anyone who had a little time. I always had the door open and made sure I was close by so I could hear him.

This particular, I heard him say "Hello, where are you going?"

And a little voice replied "To the park. Are you coming?"

I raced out to make sure that Liam wasn't going anywhere and saw Gloria with her grandson.

"Hi" I said brightly "Are you off to the park?" I hardly had the energy for Gloria so I made sure it was her grandson I was talking to

"Yes, we are" Gloria snapped "and I can't manage another one"

"I wasn't asking," I stammered in absolute shock "I only came out to make sure that Liam didn't follow you."

"To try and find a babysitter you mean." she said under her breath, and started to march away, all the while with her grandson pleading for Liam to join them.

Liam was distraught and as I picked him up and cuddled him to me, I was determined not to let her spoil our day so I packed us a drink and some sweets and we went to the park for a play on the swings. We ended up having a lovely time and although Liam soon forgot how horrible Gloria had been to him, I didn't.

For the next few months, things carried on just as horribly.

To this day, I don't know why Gloria took against me in the way that she did, but she did everything she could to belittle me and make me feel like an outsider. If I was buying a drink in the shop and there was anyone else there, she'd make a comment like "You only brought one yesterday" and would ignore my children all the time.

Luke came home from school one day in a terrible state. I asked what was wrong, he didn't want to tell me because I'd be upset. Eventually I managed to get him to open up and he told me that he'd been picked on at school for having fleas. Some kids from the estate were calling him and our family dirty and saying that we, and our house, were riddled with fleas. I couldn't believe it. Luke had never had any problems at school so where had it come from?

I asked him who had said it and when he told me, I knew the mum of the child in question quite well so I asked her very nicely the next morning. She told me that he'd overheard Gloria from the shop telling someone else that I'd been in buying things to get rid of all of the fleas in our house.

On the night of his thirteenth birthday, the situation got too much for Luke, and he broke down on me, telling me he didn't want to live there anymore!

The situation was horrible and worst of all, James didn't believe me when I told him how bad things were. He thought that, as usual, I was creating a drama out of nothing – so only Luke and I knew what was happening and were effectively on our own.

It may seem childish looking from the outside but I was distraught over the whole situation and slowly it wore me down. Day by day things got worse and inside it was torture. I already had low self-confidence, self-esteem and felt insecure but now I felt powerless even around my own family. With James not believing a word I said I struggled more and more. I had nothing to fight back with, the only thing I had was alcohol. The drink made me feel strong and invincible and when faced with Gloria, I needed it more than ever.

A few weeks passed and she carried on being just as vile but one afternoon when I was coming back from the park with the children, things came to a head. Gloria's shop was the first thing we saw when we turned the corner into our estate and I saw a group of neighbours standing outside. I wondered what was going on and then saw one woman striding towards me.

Gloria was standing outside the shop, pointing her towards

me and smiling smugly. Then she crossed her arms and watched as the woman began to shout at me.

At first I didn't know what she was saying but then she told me that she knew I'd been gossiping about her and her family. Of course I hadn't. I only knew that her name was Melanie and other than that I hadn't a clue who she was but she wouldn't listen to me. She said she knew that I'd been slating her behind her back.

I knew from what she was saying that this could have only come from one person and that was Gloria but of course she wouldn't believe me.

That was it for me. I'd had enough of this woman and her lies about my family so I looked past Melanie and told Gloria to come over. As she stormed towards me I told her loudly "I know what you're doing and it stops now."

She started screaming and swearing at me and although she wasn't making any sense I saw red and flew at her and punched her. She fought back and Luke ended up having to separate the two of us. I was so angry and although I know there is no excuse for violence, I just saw red and in the heat of the moment I lashed out. Sober, it's the last thing I would want to do in front of my children.

After that, there were no more pretences, and no more being nice to each other's faces; this was all out war and it was going to get much worse.

Chapter 19

I could still hear noise outside as I put the security chain on the front door. I felt a little safer once inside my own home. I peered through the window and saw Gloria surrounded by our neighbours – no doubt filling their heads with more lies about me. She was smiling and laughing the whole time, basking in her glory and the chaos she'd created.

I wanted to go back outside and set the record straight, but I knew I couldn't. I felt so alone and didn't have anyone to talk to. James was at work and I didn't want to disturb him.

I had nothing to do but, try to calm down. I could feel the adrenaline pumping and felt so angry. Then as I looked through the window, I could see that the crowd was getting bigger and I started to feel afraid too – the children were upstairs and I didn't want them upset.

By that point, I was getting really frightened and I didn't feel that we were safe in the house so there was nothing I could do but ring James at work and tell him what was going on. I knew he wouldn't be thrilled but I wasn't expecting him to go mad at me.

"Wherever you go, trouble follows" he shouted at me and refused to believe me when I said that I hadn't done anything.

Once James was finished shouting he slammed the phone down and I knew I needed a drink. I didn't have anything in the house but looking at the crowd outside, there was no way I could leave, I felt terrified. I felt trapped in my own home, without anything to drink or any way of getting out.

I called Alison to ask for help. She came straight over and as soon as she pulled up outside our house, the crowd disappeared and Gloria walked back into her shop.

Shakily I unhooked the chain to open the door and let her in. I told her everything, she was furious but helped to calm me down. She told me what I probably already knew... I needed to just ignore Gloria and not have anything to do with her. Alison couldn't understand why I'd want to carry on using her shop either. She was completely right and I told myself I'd never set foot in there again. Then like a true friend she told me that she was always there for me. And true to her word she has.

Eventually Alison had to go home and I was left alone again. With a neighbour I hated and a husband who seemed to detest me. I felt so sad and low.

A few days later, bright and early in the morning, I heard a commotion outside our house. I looked out and saw Gloria with her daughter and another woman standing right outside my front window. They were laughing and pointing at our house and although I didn't catch what they were saying, it was obvious I was the subject.

The way they were acting was making me really nervous and although I knew I had to leave the house shortly, I felt as though I didn't want to. I certainly didn't want to have to walk past them.

The noise had disturbed Luke so I went to pull him away from the window but by this point Gloria knew she had an audience and she started shouting abuse at the house, screaming "You dirty alcoholic" up to our window and then telling neighbours as they walked past "Did you know her kids are riddled with fleas?" Then with one last parting shot of "Dirty, skanky family," she marched down the road with her arms folded tightly.

I couldn't stand it anymore and as soon as they'd gone, I broke down in floods of tears. The kids were all upset too and we all hugged together, with them telling me that they didn't like Gloria anymore either.

I couldn't stay there a second longer and packed some bags for me and the children. Then I told James that we were going to stay with Alison for a few days. He could hear how upset the children were and I think he finally started to see what was going on.

He suggested we should all go away for the weekend to give us some space from Gloria and to get away from it all. I felt so relieved and loved the idea. We found a nice, cheap caravan site online that wasn't too far away.

Once it was all booked, I started to pack for our little break. We were only staying for two nights but it was just enough to make me feel like some of our problems had gone away. I felt free from everything and could feel the weight starting to lift. I even decided not to get too drunk as I didn't want to ruin the next day. I knew the kids were going to enjoy every minute of their break so I put all the horrible thoughts to the back of my mind.

The caravan park was lovely. There was a playground where the children could play and a clubhouse with entertainment and a disco too. For the first time in months, we were together as a family and it felt perfect.

We even managed to go the whole weekend without having a serious argument.

We arrived home on the Sunday afternoon and I was looking forward to a drink. I told James I was going to the shop to get a bottle, he pulled a face straight away so I asked what was wrong. He couldn't believe I was going to Gloria's shop after everything I'd told him. I was in no mood to be argued with, especially as I'd felt so happy. Without thinking I snapped at him that I had no intention of going to Gloria's shop and I could go wherever I wanted.

We had a row and I stormed out, taking my purse with me. I walked to the supermarket, bought a bottle of vodka and took it down to the park. I was just about to open it when I heard a voice call my name.

I thought it was James at first and turned around with gritted teeth, only to see a man I'd seen at the school gates. Chris had a daughter the same age as Liam. I remember James chatting with him before.

He walked up to me and asked what I was doing. I got a little flustered as I was sober and told him James and I had had a row and I was just calming down.

He smiled and held out a cigarette for me, saying "We've all got nagging other halves, but don't sit in the park like a wino. Come to the pub with me."

For some reason, I found myself wanting to follow him. I wasn't a big pub drinker normally. Pub prices were expensive and I preferred drinking at home where I could make my own drinks as strong as I wanted.

Still, the lure of someone who wasn't shouting at me or nagging was very appealing so I agreed to go with Chris.

I told him that James wasn't a big drinker and that we'd had a bit of a falling out. I don't know why I was telling this virtual stranger the ins and outs of our argument but for some reason I felt I could talk to him about anything. I felt calm in is company. We walked into the bar and as we went across to the bar he said "Hi" to just about everybody. He ordered us both a drink and we went to sit outside.

"You know everyone." I laughed

"Yeah" he smiled "we all know each other in here. We're like a little family when the real ones get too boring."

I know now that Chris was just like me. He had a drinking problem too and probably had a family who cared about him and wanted him to stop. From meetings with Alcoholics Anonymous I've learned that addicts tend to surround themselves with other addicts because they can validate each other's' behaviour. There aren't any real friendships there but they're able to look around a crowded pub or party and tell themselves that if there are this many people acting like them then they can't be doing anything wrong.

I trusted Chris immediately, he was telling me everything I wanted to hear.

We carried on drinking and after a while, he bought some shots of vodka. The last thing I remember is downing them one after the other and feeling his hand on my thigh.

I woke up the following morning lying on my sofa fully clothed with my head feeling like it was about to split open.

Once again, I couldn't recall my evening; I had a strange feeling and thought something must have happened. When I went to the bathroom I was right, my neck and chest was covered in love bites.

I was horrified and still with evidence on my body, I had no recollection of the night before. I was getting more and more flustered by the second. I spent the whole week feeling awful. I still had no idea what exactly had happened and all James said was that I'd staggered through the door after eleven looking dishevelled, which wasn't unusual. I'd told him I'd been at the park and had passed out on the sofa where he'd left me.

I had cheated on James before, but never like this. We'd been separated at the time and I'd never actually had to lie to him.

This felt different and I felt dirty and disgusted with myself. I had betrayed James and the children once again and it didn't matter how many times I showered, I couldn't get the feeling of Chris' hand on my thigh to go away.

I spent the next few days hoping that James wouldn't get too close and locking the bathroom or bedroom door whenever I had to get changed so that nobody noticed the bites.

I felt sick every time I looked in the mirror. I was so scared of what I'd done and what James would do if he found out. So I did what I always did to escape; I drank.

The more I drank the more the guilt set in, but rather than focus the guilt, and the anger it created, where it belonged, I started to take my anger out on James.

We ended up having another furious row and the police were called. The police arriving to settle or break up one of our arguments wasn't out of the ordinary, so much so that Social Services were also well aware of how volatile our house was now.

Their knock on the door scared me and I got it into my head that they had brought big dogs to attack me. Terrified, I ran into the back garden lying on the grass and telling myself that if I was really still they wouldn't be able to see me.

When I describe myself lying in the middle of our small garden in the dark, hiding, it sounds quite funny but at the time I was terrified. I was so paranoid when I was drinking that by now I was imagining threats and seeing things that weren't there. I'm sure it's just another consequence of mixing alcohol and the medication I was on, but at the time I was paralysed by fear.

Of course they found me, and one look at James covered in bruises and cuts from our argument convinced them I needed a night in the cells. I was arrested for being Drunk and

Disorderly and taken off to sober up for the night.

Before they let me go the next morning, they told me that an urgent referral to Social Services had been made for the children.

As well as feeling totally ashamed that Social Services were now involved on an official basis, I felt angry. I hated the world and felt that everyone and everything was against me, and now I had spies watching our every move. To be honest, at that time it never occurred to me that they might be there to take the children. I just viewed them as a pest. I was wrong.

I went home in tears and tried to make things right with James but the atmosphere in the house was awful. James wouldn't even speak to me, and didn't for a few days. Alison kept visiting to make sure we were okay and I was still escaping to the pub whenever I could but things were starting to build up again and I was feeling severely depressed.

After a horrible but uneventful week, I saw Gloria walking past our house. Our lovely cat was walking just in front of her and as he walked past her she aimed her foot at him; kicking him viciously. I wanted desperately to go outside and retaliate but knew that I'd just make things worse if I did.

So, I just drank until James came home. The second he walked through the door, I told him exactly what had happened and he was so angry with Gloria that he didn't notice how drunk I was.

He'd passed her on his way into the house as she was standing outside the shop smoking and when he heard what I had to tell him, he stormed back outside and demanded to know what she'd done.

Just as she had with me, she responded by screeching and swearing at him. She went to kick him and although he dodged her, I could see that it was taking all of his strength not to retaliate.

Just as things looked as though they were about to get much worse, Alison pulled up and luckily, she saw what was going on. Knowing what Gloria could be like, Alison grabbed James by the shoulder and luckily had the strength to pull him away. Then she marched up to Gloria to give her a piece of her mind. Like all bullies, Gloria wasn't keen on being stood up to and she quickly scuttled back inside the shop.

James might have been too angry with Gloria to notice the state I was in when he came home from work but once he and Alison came in after this incident, he soon did. He saw it was only four in the afternoon and absolutely erupted!

He shouted, none of his friends had the drama of coming home to a drunken state of a wife and that enough was enough. He yelled at me to Get Out!

Alison knew that she had to get me away from there as soon as possible and said that I could stay with her. She sent me upstairs to pack a bag and we climbed into her car. Liam had insisted that he wanted to come with us and so Alison promised James that she'd look after him as well as me and we left.

As we drove off, I could see Gloria standing outside the shop again looking delighted that she'd managed to cause an almighty row in my family.

Alison didn't have any alcohol at her place so I begged her to stop on the way to get me some vodka, wisely she refused and said I needed to think clearly. So I spent the night sobering up and trying to work out what I could do. I woke up and felt confused that I couldn't find Liam. I must have looked really puzzled as Alison asked what was wrong. Because I was so drunk the night before, I was only half-sure that we'd brought Liam with us and when I asked her, she answered quickly that he'd wanted to go home to James and she'd taken him. She sounded convincing and so I never questioned her beyond that.

Later on, Alison told me the truth. I had upset Liam to the point that he had to be taken back to James. He was trying to talk to me but I was so drunk and upset that I'd put my hand over his mouth quite roughly. I'd blocked his mouth and nose for a few seconds and had frightened him. Alison had been sure at the time that I wasn't trying to deliberately hurt him but nevertheless I had.

Of all my children, Liam is the most sensitive and it makes me sick to my stomach that I could have hurt him during my drinking. I knew that I'd been violent to James but when Alison told me this I felt utterly ashamed of myself and horrified that that part of me existed. I knew that I had to ask James to be completely honest with me and tell me if I'd ever hurt the children other than that occasion. James and I have a pact now to be completely honest with each other and so he told me that although I never hit any of the children, I was rough with Luke on more than one occasion. I couldn't believe it when I heard him say that I would shout and swear at Luke and on some occasions I would even spit at him. I feel so ashamed of myself.

I can never excuse or take away what I've done but if ever I needed a reminder to stay sober, this is it. It's easy to forget that it wasn't just me who was affected by my drinking. My whole family suffered, they too paid the price of living with an alcoholic. Although I am more than a hundred per cent certain that I'll never drink again, I've made James swear that if I did, he would take the children away from me.

At the time, I didn't have that clarity and so the next morning I told Alison I'd had enough of James and him controlling me. I was sick of Gloria and her bullying and I was sick of that vile street. I asked her to take me to the council offices where I would get a house for me and the children away from all of our troubles.

I waited for hours at the council offices to see the right person and when I was finally called in, the news wasn't what I wanted to hear. As James had sorted our new house out while I was in hospital it was in his name. Because the children had a home, the only thing they could offer me was a one bedroom flat on my own. I wasn't having any of it; the children were my world and I wasn't going anywhere without them. This of course meant that I'd have to go home.

I had no choice but to go back and I waited nervously for James. As I was waiting, a man from Social Services turned up. They'd received the Police referral and were coming to collect details. He introduced himself as Peter and was really nice to me, explaining what was happening and what it all meant.

Peter said that he'd been assigned to our family and would be working with us to get a safe situation for the children. For the moment though they were being put on the "in need" register.

That meant that I would be having regular visits to check on me, that James and I couldn't have any more arguments and that if there were any more drunken incidents we would end up losing the children.

I was at my wits end. My children meant the earth to me, and I loved them more than anything; there was no way I could face losing them again.

I hated the fact Social Services were involved. I had no choice but to comply with what they said.

From the beginning though, there was something about Peter that I trusted. He was never anything other than honest about being there to protect the children but whenever he could, he did his best to help me too.

Between trying to keep things together for the children and doing what Social Services wanted, I was really struggling with the guilt of my one night stand with Chris. It was eating me up inside and I knew I had to tell someone, so I wrote a long email to Alison telling her what I could remember and what I thought had happened.

I was surprised to get a call from her straight away. She was furious with me and said I had to tell James. She was worried if he heard it from anyone else, he would be devastated and embarrassed. I knew she was right and when I remembered that James and Chris had spoken in the playground while collecting our children from school, the bile rose in my throat and I felt sickened.

So I asked Alison if she would come and take the children out for a walk just before James was due home from work. Like any true friend she did and offered to help me to sort things out if she could. Then I poured myself a drink for courage and waited for James.

By the time he got home, I felt so nervous that I practically yelled at James what happened. He collapsed onto the sofa and wept as he asked me to tell him the details I could remember. Of course, the only thing I could remember was a hand on my thigh and then waking up with the love bites. James asked me to show them to him and realised that I'd been covering them all week.

Then he yelled at me, calling me names and telling me that once and for all, our marriage was over.

By the time Alison came back with the children, I was sitting on the step with a bag James had made me pack. As Alison walked up the street James came outside to take the children. Luke and Liam went straight with him but Ami wouldn't let go of me. As he tried to coax her inside she kept shouting, "No, I want Mummy. I want my mummy." Eventually and with tears in his eyes, he told me to look after her and went inside where I could hear Liam sobbing for me and his sister.

Alison offered for us to stay at her house until we could get ourselves sorted but this time I refused. I didn't want anyone else to get caught up in our mess anymore, so I said I would go and stay at a B & B in Tonbridge, a nearby town. Because I was known to the local council and had already been turned down by them, I knew we'd need to be a bit further away if we stood a chance to get emergency accommodation.

Alison reluctantly dropped us off in Tonbridge and we walked to the B & B. I'd seen this particular guest house before and knew their rates were cheap. I'd always had it in the back of my mind as an emergency escape if things got so bad with James that I couldn't stay or if Social Services had asked me to leave.

I was in such a state that it never occurred to me to call in advance to check if they had any vacancies. I simply knocked on the door and asked if they had a room free. Luckily, there were and after paying, Ami and I made our way upstairs.

I was trying to keep her as calm as I could so I made out that we were on a little holiday like the ones we used to take when we lived in Southend.

Once we were settled, we went to find a shop so that I could buy us some food. I knew we'd have to be careful with money and because we needed to go to the council offices the following day, for the first time in a long time, I didn't have a drink that night.

Chapter 20

The following morning was a blur but I can clearly remember that my stomach was tight and full of butterflies. The rational part of me kept telling me to ring Alison and ask her to come and collect Ami. She could then tell James to collect her from there. It wasn't Ami's fault that I'd done what I'd done and I shouldn't have dragged her along with me, but having her there meant I had to be strong and face reality rather than doing what I wanted to do which was to lock myself in a dark room with a large bottle.

And so we left the B&B and I tried to keep calm. I had no idea where we were going but I knew that I had to stay focused. I did my best to keep my cool, even if it was just for show so Ami didn't get upset.

I took Ami to McDonalds for breakfast and then into a toyshop to buy her a present for being so good for me and to distract her while I got us sorted out. She chose a plastic Tinkerbell laptop for ten pound; Ami was happy which really helped me too. We then made our way to Tonbridge council offices.

We arrived around ten in the morning, completed our registration then sat in the waiting room and waited until we were called to speak with the appropriate housing officer. It took all morning. That gave me a lot of time to think and I went into a panic. I was both terrified and full of regret. I felt so alone and scared, my life was a shambles. My phone had completely run out of battery and so I couldn't even get hold of anyone and nobody could contact us.

We were finally seen around one in the afternoon. After visiting Maidstone Council offices, I assumed they wouldn't be able to give us anywhere to stay. With that in mind I knew I had to tell this housing officer a different story, so I lied and said that we were fleeing domestic violence. I knew that it was a horrible thing to do but I felt I had no other choice.

The lady who saw us was lovely. She really wanted to help us and I completely broke down. As far as she knew, I was crying over James and the situation I'd told her about but in reality it was a situation I'd created and only I was to blame. She told me she'd try her hardest to help us but we would have to wait while they made arrangements.

Ami was brilliantly behaved throughout the whole day and the laptop I'd bought for her really helped to distract her. Soon though, we were hungry and so we left the offices briefly to get some lunch.

I knew by that point that I really needed to start being careful with my money. We only had what was in the bank to live on and that was very little. I wasn't very good at managing finances at the best of times, but by that point the medication I was taking for my Bipolar Disorder was being washed away with the alcohol and so I was back to reckless spending. I should have known at the time from both the spending and what I had done with Chris that I was ill, but I was blind to it all, the vodka was in charge and I wasn't thinking rationally.

After we'd eaten we went back to the council offices and waited until four pm when the Domestic Violence Officer could speak to us. I had another long interview where I had to give all the details about our situation, it was simply lie after lie, but I was desperate for somewhere for Ami and I to live. It was turning into a very long day where I felt exhausted and drained!

At the end of their working day the council staff went home and we were left in the waiting room, the doors were locked and we still sat there waiting, unsure where my life was heading, scared and alone with my thoughts. A kind security guard had taken a shine to Ami who was now exhausted. He kept checking on us and telling us that it wouldn't be long now.

Eventually, he came through to collect us. He'd had a message to say they were ready and he took us through to an office where we were to wait. He fetched a box of toys and gave them to Ami and then left us to wait.

A few minutes later a lady came in to us. She sat opposite me and told me that she thought she could help but that there were lots of forms to fill in.

She explained that she knew Social Services were involved with our family and that they'd been working with them that day to find a solution and some emergency housing.

I'd later find out that once they realised I was in sole charge of Ami they made moves to have an emergency order to remove her from my care.

I thought it was odd at the time that she wasn't asking too much about my situation with James and seemed to be taking a lot of what I said at face value. I also know now that she had been in contact with the mental health team who had expressed their concerns about my welfare and were preparing an intervention.

I don't know if it was her job to distract me with emergency accommodation or to make me feel secure for Ami's safety but she offered us a house in a local area. She guided me through a few forms for council tax and housing benefit and said that someone from her office would be out to see me very soon.

She spent the rest of the interview telling us about the house. Because I had a small child with me, they had to ensure that what they offered us was suitable. In this case, the house was fully furnished and although we had nothing, it had beds, a sofa and a fitted kitchen.

I couldn't believe it. For the whole day I'd been dreading the night time. I had visions of Ami and I in a hostel or another shelter, and what I wanted more than anything was to wake up and find that this had all been a horrible nightmare. The day had been filled with darkness but being told that we had somewhere to go, where I could take Ami and know that she would be safe and comfortable felt like a glimmer of light. It was far more than I deserved.

She gave me the keys to our new home and directions. Luckily we didn't have far to go and after thanking the lady, and crying a lot more, I took Ami's hand and we left.

As we stepped out of the council offices, the cold air hit us and I held onto Ami's hand tightly, telling her that we'd be okay as long as we were together. I think I was trying to reassure myself more than anything. I followed the directions given to me and although I was nervous about what we were going to find when we arrived, I didn't want to show Ami my nervousness. I kept my voice as bright as I could and tried to make it all seem like an adventure, while deep down inside I was shaking like a leaf and frightened.

We'd only been outside for a minute when I saw a car pull in by us. The headlights were flashing and the driver sounded the horn loudly. I looked around to see but I didn't know anyone in Tonbridge so I thought they couldn't be for me. It was difficult to see into the car and thought the driver must have made a mistake so we carried on walking. I felt nervous as we walked, I'd upset a lot of people through my behaviour and I was praying that this wasn't someone who had come to retaliate. I had Ami with me and was worried for her.

I tried to look inside the car as it drove past and thought I could make out two figures. They were waving furiously and trying to get my attention but I kept my head down and told Ami we needed to hurry up as our new home was waiting for us.

They pulled into a lay-by and I saw someone get out. My heart was pounding and I was scared wondering what was going to happen. Then I saw a child get out of the car. I was stunned as I saw that it was my little Liam running towards me screaming "Mummy." He practically jumped into my arms and held on tightly. I looked past him and realised that the man with him was Peter, our Social Worker.

I felt utterly confused. I didn't know that Peter knew where I was and I couldn't believe he'd brought Liam out so late on such a cold night.

He caught up and smiled kindly. Then he explained that Liam had been getting into a state not knowing where I was. He wanted to know that I was safe, and so did Peter.

Liam was crying the whole time he was hugging me, and kept begging Peter to let him stay. Peter shook his head and said very seriously "No Liam, you have to come back to Daddy with me I'm afraid." I wanted to beg him for Liam to stay with us, but the tone of his voice made me afraid to.

We'd only been there for a few minutes when Peter told Liam it was time to go home now. He told me he'd be in touch the following day to talk to me privately about everything that had happened. Liam was devastated and Peter had to wrench him away from me. Ami had started crying and I was sobbing too.

It never made sense to me at the time why Peter would bring Liam to me, knowing how much it would upset us all. It was like he had been deliberately cruel.

It took me a while to see that this was Peters' last ditch attempt to make me see sense. If he could show me how devastated Liam was then maybe I'd snap out of what I was doing and do the right thing for my children. I believe that Peter really cared about our family and this was his way of going above and beyond his duty as our family Social Worker. Had it not been for him working with our family I dread to think what might have happened as another person might not have seen me as kindly as Peter had.

Peter must have known that the following morning he'd be preparing an emergency care order to have Ami taken away from me as well.

But still, he had to take Liam that night. He carried him back to the car, and the whole time Liam was struggling and screaming to come back to me. I could hear him crying "I want my Mummy" and my heart broke. I stood in the street crying for my little boy and comforted Ami as she cried for him to come back.

They couldn't and didn't come back and I knew I had to get Ami to our house as soon as possible. She was exhausted.

I stopped by a little supermarket on the way as we didn't have any food or drink. I walked around in a daze, throwing things into a basket. Ami asked if she could have a few things and I just put them in without even checking the price, or what she was having. I do remember that I picked up a pretty cardigan and put it into the basket for her.

Then we got to the drinks aisle. I had Ami with me and shouldn't have even considered having a drink but as I was still shaking from seeing Liam I knew I needed something to calm my nerves. I grabbed a bottle of vodka and promised myself that I wouldn't open it until I'd settled her off to sleep.

Once we'd finished in the supermarket, we went back out into the cold night to find our new home. I got really lost and had to keep stopping to ask for directions but Ami carried on walking and kept us both going. Finally we arrived.

It was furnished, just as they lady had said, but it wasn't nice at all. All the walls and furniture had burn marks on them and there was a pungent smell of burning, urine, stale smoke and body odour. It was just vile and I was convinced it must have been used for drugs before we got it. Had I been alone, I wouldn't have minded but I was seeing it through Ami's eyes and it was just no place for her. She deserved to be at home with her brothers and her Daddy, tucked up in her nice warm bed, but instead she was in a horrible situation I had created.

I knew that she shouldn't be here, but for tonight we had no option. I tried to make it an adventure for her, so we went exploring. We found a bathroom, a bedroom and a kitchen. Clearly, the council had known that we didn't have anything with us and had left an emergency hamper with milk, shampoo, dry foods and some towels.

Ami's tiredness had caught up with her so I took her upstairs and let her fall asleep in my arms. She'd had such a long and tiring day yet she'd been an angel. I was so proud of her and kept whispering to her, telling her how much I loved her and how proud I was of her.

After she'd settled off to sleep, I went back into the kitchen to unpack the things we'd bought and to pour myself a drink. I sat downstairs finally alone with my thoughts.

After the day we'd had, I just wanted to lose myself in oblivion but I was so tired that I had just a few drinks and took myself off to bed.

Chapter 21

The next morning, I woke up confused. Almost like a bad dream that had turned out to be real. Ami was still fast asleep and I lay next to her trying not to panic.

I looked up at the disgusting ceiling and knew in my heart that I had done the wrong thing bringing Ami into this. I should have done the sensible thing and left her with Alison so that James could take her home, but I'd been scared and clung to her. Today I couldn't let that fear take over again. I had to start making good decisions, if not for me then for Ami. She was innocent and she didn't deserve this horrible situation that I'd plunged her into. I had pushed everyone but her away with my horrific behaviour and before it was too late, I needed to put things right for her.

I knew what I had to do, which was to give her back to James, so I went into auto-pilot. I knew that if I started thinking too much about what I was doing then I wouldn't find the strength to go through with it. So I got myself dressed and then woke Ami up. I told her we were going out for breakfast and walked into town.

I was in a rough area and I felt intimidated. I held onto her hand tightly and watched as people made their way to school and work. Ami looked so tiny skipping along and I knew, once again that she truly didn't belong here with me. She should be on her way to school or at home chatting to James, and I would make sure she got back there.

Feeling horrible; and very sorry for myself all I wanted to do was to drink until I could forget what was going on. The problem was that this situation wasn't going away. The first thing on my 'To do' list, was to buy a new mobile phone charger. My battery had been dead for about two days now and it was time I faced the world again. Then Ami and I had some breakfast and went back to the flat.

Just as I'd thought, I had loads of text and voice messages. Most of them were from James who sounded furious with me. I listened to them, shaking. A few minutes later, it rang. It was James and I braced myself as I answered. As expected, he was now, well beyond angry. He was screaming at me, demanding to know where we were. I let him rant at me, knowing that he had every right to, and then told him we were in Tonbridge and asked him to come and collect Ami. He wanted to know the address but I was planning on staying and wanted a clean break so I told him I would meet him around the corner from where I was.

I didn't tell him that I was planning on giving Ami back to him permanently but I suppose that looking back, I never had a choice in that anyway. What mattered at the time was that Ami was going home and would be safe and happy.

I told Ami that she was going to see Daddy, Luke and Liam and tried to get her excited. I told her it was only for a few days while I got our house nice for us to live in and, although I knew I was telling her a lie at the time, I also knew that it was for the best.

The whole time, I was trying not to fall apart. I was shaking and was so upset, yet somehow I managed to keep my voice even.

James had left straight away, I knew he had been frantic and wanted Ami with him as soon as possible so I set out with her. Our meeting point was opposite some shops and it was a very intimidating place. Late morning and already there were a big group of teenage boys outside, smoking and shouting at passing cars and I could feel that Ami was nervous, so I scooped her up and waited for James.

As we stood there, I could feel my heart breaking but I knew that I had to be strong. I knew what a fantastic dad James was and how much he loved the children so I knew she'd be completely safe and secure. She was looking forward to seeing everyone at home and I carried on telling here that it would just be for a few days and I'd be back with her.

Whatever I'd done in the past I had always wanted the children with me. I loved them fiercely and with every breath I had and although I might not have shown it, I really did want the very best for them. Handing Ami back to James then, especially when I'd already lost Luke and Liam was the hardest thing I'd ever had to do but the truth is that I had no fight left in me.

Everything that had gone wrong for us was my fault. I had broken everyone's hearts and now it was time to start putting things right, even if that meant breaking mine. I was empty, numb and broken and I didn't deserve anyone or anything. It was time to face up to what I'd done, and the only way to do that was to do it alone.

James soon arrived and I knew from the second he pulled up that he was different. He looked broken, yet angry and determined; as he stepped out of the car I knew we were going to have an argument. He pulled Ami into a cuddle and put her safely in the car. He went to the back of the car, pulled out a suitcase and a holdall and threw them into the road.

He told me that was everything of mine and I handed him Ami's things wordlessly. I knew that if I tried to speak to him then I would just break down and I couldn't do that. I just wanted to get back to the flat.

He wasn't ready for me to go though. He started to yell at me, giving me a full tirade of how he felt. I can't remember what he said exactly, only that he was furious with me. He had every right to be and what stuck out more than what he was saying, was how different he looked. I do remember him telling me that I had lost him for good. He screamed at me to realise what the drink was turning me into and screamed at me to see what a huge problem I had. Then he told me I had made my bed and now I had to lie in it.

My resolve was starting to break and I knew that I couldn't handle staying there any longer so I picked up the cases, turned around and walked away as fast as I could. I took one last look at Ami who was crying and screaming in the car and then stared at the floor. I didn't look up at the crowd who had been staring at us, or the teenagers standing outside the shop jeering. I didn't look at the car as it sped past, even though I could still hear Ami crying. I didn't dare move my eyes away from the pavement until I reached the flat.

I locked the door behind me and yanked the curtains closed.

When I was finally alone and had shut out the outside world, I started to panic. I had finally lost my children for good and I couldn't cope with the idea that I might never see them again.

Trying to stay focused I knew I had to keep busy, so I decided to unpack the suitcase James had brought for me. I carried it upstairs and laid it out on the bed and opened it.

At the top of the suitcase James had packed photographs of us all in happier times. It was more than I could cope with and I turned them over so that I didn't have to look at the smiling faces, and decided I needed a drink.

I poured myself a large straight vodka and downed it in one. As I felt the familiar buzz and the numbness it brought, my problems started to drift away, and I carried on drinking as I unpacked.

It wasn't long before I was tired and drunk and soon fell asleep on the bed for a few hours but waking up in the strange environment put me into a panic again and as I stared around the empty room and felt the full weight of the silence. I felt sure the only way I was going to stay calm was to keep on drinking.

I drank for the next few hours until I heard the doorbell ring. I was quite drunk and put the bottle under my bed before I went to answer the door.

It was Peter; our social worker. I trusted him, and as I've already said, I strongly believe that he really cared about doing the best for our family.

I invited him in and he told me he knew that I'd handed Ami over to James. Then he explained that as I'd handed the children over to James I didn't need to be on his case load any more. He went on to explain they had planned to intervene and put Ami into James' care but as I'd handed her over myself they no longer needed to take action.

Then he looked me straight in the eye and asked me to be honest with him. I agreed.

"Have you been drinking?" he asked

I looked to the floor and replied honestly "Yes."

"How much have you had?"

"I don't know."

"Can I see the bottle?" he asked

I took him upstairs and pulled the bottle from underneath the bed and passed it to him.

He nodded and asked if I would go back downstairs for a chat with him.

"Why was the bottle hidden under your bed?"

I didn't understand what he meant so he asked again. Now that I lived alone, I had no reason to hide the bottle so why had I?

I had no idea but the question made me stop and think. I had nobody to answer to and nobody to lie to so why had I hidden the bottle. Peter told me that he knew the answer and explained that hiding the bottle was a metaphor for hiding the problem. It's something that a lot of alcoholics do, whether they have someone checking up on them or not.

As I've thought about it, this was typical behaviour for me. I'd finish a bottle and wouldn't want anyone to find it so rather than throwing it in the bin, I'd hide it around the house. I was always terrified that if James found an empty bottle in the bin then he'd decided I'd had enough and wouldn't let me open any more. I used to hide half full bottles too, thinking that if he refused to let me buy any I'd at least have a stash hidden somewhere.

James never knew I was hiding my bottles until earlier that morning when he'd started to pack my things. He'd found an empty bottle inside the wardrobe and had realised what I'd been doing.

Then he'd searched through the bedroom. By the time he'd been through the wardrobes, cupboards, drawers and under the bed, he'd found nineteen empty vodka bottles.

As he told me this I realised just how much I had been hiding the truth from myself as well as everyone else.

Peter said he could get me to a clinic so that I could get the help I needed and thought I needed to go. I listened as he explained that because he wasn't classed as my social worker any more, I would have to go voluntarily.

I remember feeling so grateful to Peter for his kindness. I believed most people in his position would have turned their back on me, especially as I wasn't even on his case load but he cared enough to still try to help, and I will forever be grateful for his kindness.

I sat and thought about it. The only thing right now taking away the pain I felt was the vodka and I couldn't cope without it so I said no and refused Peter's offer.

Peter nodded and told me he had to leave but would always be there if I needed him. He left me with his number and I was alone again.

Not long after, Alison called me. She'd spoken to James and knew everything that happened. She was calling to check I was okay and was trying to arrange to come and see me but after Peter had left I'd carried on drinking. I hadn't eaten anything since breakfast with Ami and so I just got drunker and drunker and can't remember much about the conversation I had with her, only that she was promising to see me soon.

Once I was off the phone, I staggered upstairs and passed out on the bed. I woke the next morning; sober. I forced myself out of bed and stumbled down to the kitchen. I'd run out of vodka the night before so I pulled my clothes on and rushed out the door to find the nearest shop. I didn't care about my reflection or how I must have looked. I had a mission and that was all that mattered. It's a scary thought that some mornings while I was drinking I didn't even look in the mirror or bother to brush my hair. I didn't care about my appearance and must have looked horrific. It could be weeks between washing my hair or making sure I looked okay but the addiction took over to the point that my appearance no longer mattered.

I found the closest off-licence that was open, I had no appetite so I picked up a few energy drinks. I'd used them to line my stomach before and as well as giving me a little boost when I was feeling tired, they also helped me to handle what I was drinking. I found I was less likely to vomit if I'd had a few of these drinks and as I really hated being sick; that was a bonus in itself.

I asked for a large bottle of vodka, the shopkeeper looked at me strangely but still rang the bottle through along with the other drinks.

I marched back to the flat and twisted the top off the bottle. I drank straight from the bottle, desperate to obliterate my thoughts.

When I first started drinking, I had wanted the confidence it gave me. I felt shy and awkward but with a drink I was dynamic and interesting, or so I thought.

After a while, my reasons for drinking had changed and now I just drank to forget. The more I drank, the easier it was to forget what else was happening in my life.

The problem was that even this wasn't working. I was trapped in a never ending cycle of drinking my problems away and then waking up with even more because of the things I'd done while I was drunk. Now, the only break I got from those problems was when I slept. I could never recall any dreams, so it was the only time I felt any peace and then I'd wake up sober and right back to where I started.

I didn't realise it at the time but there was nothing about my life I enjoyed. As I drank, the harsh reality of the situation set in again and the flashing images of James and the children just added to the craving and soon I was drunk again, alone with the bottle and soon I passed out.

Chapter 22

Ever since I was diagnosed with epilepsy, I've been able to tell when a seizure is about to hit me. It starts with a very powerful sensation of Deja-vu. The doctor told me it's a warning sign that I'm about to have a fit. He had explained to me that if I get this feeling, I should try to put myself in a safe position like lying or sitting down and if I'm in the bath or shower I should get out straight away, this information may well have saved my life.

Deja-vu normally lasts a few minutes, and then I lose concentration. I find it difficult to focus or speak and that goes on for about fifteen minutes.

That morning, I had all the usual symptoms and went into a "petit mal" seizure. These small seizures can sometimes be warning signs of a much bigger one to come. The difficult thing about managing epilepsy is that there's no way of telling what kind of fit you're going to have or when.

Once I came round and realised I'd had a fit, it soon dawned on me that I hadn't taken my medication for a few days. Luckily, James was still looking out for me and had packed them in my bag so I went to take them.

The doctors made it very clear that I wasn't allowed to drink while taking the medication. The tablets were strong and made me really drowsy; so drinking with them was an awful idea. That morning, I wasn't thinking at all so I washed the tablets down with a very large vodka and coke.

To be honest, I really didn't care anymore. I was drunk, alone and the silence of the flat was deafening me. I was alone with my thoughts and I hated them.

I was utterly terrified and had no idea what to do next. I couldn't see any way that anything was going to get better and as each new wave of fear hit my brain; I got more and more panicked.

I was walking round the kitchen manically, not knowing what I was doing or trying to do but feeling completely unable to stop. I kept grabbing at my glass and knocking the contents back as quickly as I could. Then I'd pour myself another drink swilling and spilling it as I did.

I'd rush to the window and that would make me cry because it wasn't the right garden; I wanted to be looking out from my family home. I looked around the room and saw a host of safety instructions, phone numbers for emergency services and helplines. What struck me was that there were no photographs or pictures. There was nothing to suggest that anyone should live here, and if I didn't belong here then where did I belong?

I was nothing; nobody and I had nothing and nobody. I had no purpose and knew I was just a washed up mess living in emergency housing with nobody to care about what I did.

It was terrifying.

Without thinking, I reached into my bag and grabbed a box of Paracetamol. I popped all of the tablets out of the box, grabbed my epilepsy medication and did the same with that and found some more painkillers and put them with the pile. By the time I'd finished there was a small pile of pills on the table in front of me.

I sat and stared at them, all the while thinking about my options. I had none. It was that simple. There was nothing left for me and yet, right there was a solution. I could end it all.

I felt calm and rational. I didn't want to talk to anybody or say anything. I didn't want to leave a letter or a note. I just simply didn't want to be here anymore. I hated myself and everything I had done. I hated the hurt I had caused and I was determined that I wouldn't cause any more.

Finally I had an option. I would die. I would simply slip away in this flat with nobody to notice or care. Everyone would be better off without me and I could become nothing but a memory.

Then a determination hit me. If I was going to do this then I was doing it right now, this second. I had no strength to start again or keep on repeating my sad cycle. I just wanted to end everyone's pain with my death.

I poured myself drink after drink and took all of the tablets, using the vodka to swallow them and block out any comprehension of what I was doing. I'm not sure how much I must have drunk but it was a full litre bottle that I'd bought from the off licence.

I must have passed out, but when I came to I was lying at the bottom of the stairs. I was totally confused and it took a few minutes for me to work out what had happened. My eyes wouldn't open properly and I couldn't remember where I was. I couldn't feel any pain and didn't know whether it was the overdose I'd taken or whether I'd knocked myself out to the point that I was really badly hurt and in shock.

I tried to stand, but my legs wouldn't work so I reached out to the table near me to pull myself up. I had no strength in my legs so instead of helping me to stand I pulled the table on top of me with a crash. In pain and terrified, I tried to scream for help but no sound came out.

All of the calm and resolve I'd felt before I'd taken the pills had gone and I was starting to feel genuinely frightened. I remember being dizzy and tired as well as really worried that my legs wouldn't hold me up.

I was still convinced that I wanted to die though. I hadn't changed my mind and although I had screamed for someone to help me, it wasn't for them to stop me. If I had someone holding my hand and sitting with me then I could die knowing I wasn't quite the awful person I believed I was. As I panicked some more, I was willing a sound, any sound, to come out of my mouth and the more I worked myself up, the more I needed to scream and shout just so that I had a release. If the last sound I heard in this world was my own voice then so be it but at least it would be a sound, rather than the deafening silence of my flat.

In a state of panic and fear, I started to hallucinate. There were people standing all around me, whispering and shouting at me. Of all of the images, one is more vivid than the others. It was a man I'd never seen before. He was sitting on the stairs above me, looking down and laughing at me. He was wearing jeans and a t-shirt and kept disappearing and then reappearing. He told me I deserved this and that he'd come to watch me die. He said he had a key to the flat and he'd keep coming back because he wanted to watch.

I pleaded with him to help me, but he kept saying no, because nobody wanted me alive. Then he'd disappear again and I'd be wondering where he went until suddenly he was there again and I'd jump in fright.

It's easy to pass what was happening off as hallucinations or a dream but at the time this was so real and the most frightening thing to ever happen to me. I kept sobbing and trying to cry out for help.

Along with the man, the other people were laughing at me and watching me. As they pointed and jeered, I started to freak out. By that point, I'd been sick and was starting to choke in my panic so I knew I had to get out of there and get some help.

I was sure that if I could just get to the front door then I'd be okay because there was an arm chair by the door that I could drag myself to and call for help.

It took all of my strength but I managed to start dragging myself along by the tops of my arms. It didn't take me long to tire out and I passed out again. When I came around, I'd vomited again and had been incontinent. I'd lost complete control of my body.

I still had my eyes closed and didn't have the strength to open them so when I heard a noise by the door I was completely confused. I tried to scream for help but again no sound would come out and when someone shouted my name through the letterbox I couldn't answer them, no matter how hard I tried.

It suddenly occurred to me that with all the lights in the flat off, and me unable to make a sound, anyone who had come to help would think nobody was in and would leave me alone.

The shouting eventually stopped and all I could hear was the silence. I wanted to cry but I didn't even have the strength to do that. I knew I had to get to the door so I carried on trying to crawl. I'd manage to get about a centimetre along the carpet before I'd get so tired that I had to stop and either rest or faint with the effort.

As the time dragged by I started to pass out again. I was going in and out of consciousness, spending less time awake and I could hear my mobile phone ringing but as it was on the other side of the room I couldn't do anything to get to it.

I have no idea how long I was here but what may have minutes felt like hours. I continued to lose and regain consciousness. I'd wake up feeling weaker and sicker. I begged for it to end and passed out again feeling helpless and hopeless.

When I came to again I heard a loud banging on the door. It sounded like there were lots of people out there. I tried again to shout for help but the effort made me lose consciousness.

The next time I came to, there was more banging on the door but this time instead of a sharp knocking it was a full hammering and someone was shining a torch through the door and window.

The next thing I knew, the torch was shining in my eyes as a policeman had kicked the door through. There were two policemen in my living room and with them was an ambulance crew.

They shouted at me, to keep me conscious and took hold of my arms and shoulders to lift me onto the sofa. The motion made me sick and I threw up everywhere.

Once on the sofa, they were asking questions. I can't remember what they were asking but only that my speech was so slurred I couldn't make them understand me. I kept trying to beg them to let me change my clothes from where I'd been sick and had wet myself but of course, they couldn't understand me so they couldn't do as I asked.

The next thing I knew I was lying in a hospital bed with James sitting beside me. He looked sad and kept shaking his head and stroking my face. To be honest, it felt like a dream. I kept drifting in and out of consciousness and I wasn't sure if he was really there or whether I was still hallucinating.

When I finally managed to stay conscious long enough to take anything in, I realised I had a drip in each arm. I couldn't speak so I hadn't been able to say anything to James, I was still slipping in and out of consciousness and before I knew it he'd disappeared.

The next time I woke, I was in a different ward.

I later found out that I'd been in hospital for four days before I regained consciousness properly. I remember fleeting bits like seeing James and hearing noises but nothing else. I was really surprised to find out that I'd been on several wards and moved around to get the right care.

The first time I have any real recollection was a few days later when I came round in a room with six other beds in. The other patients were mostly elderly and a kind looking man said to me "Oh, you're finally back in the room. It's good to see you girl."

I tried to sit up but was hit by dizziness straight away and fell back down onto the pillow. For the first time I looked down and saw that I had a drip going into my arm with several fluids coming from various bags. I also had a catheter and I was horrified by it. I had no memory of it being fitted and although it wasn't painful it was uncomfortable having it there. All I knew was that I wanted it out of me and as soon as possible.

Having noticed that I was awake a nurse came in to see me. She started to do my observations and as she was taking my blood pressure and temperature, she was asking me lots of questions but I still couldn't speak. She carried on though, almost as though she was trying to coax me into answering or communicating with her. I had lots of questions for her as well. I wanted to know where I was, how long had I been there, what was wrong with me, was I going to be okay? But it didn't seem to matter how much I tried. I couldn't speak and she couldn't understand me.

I started to fear the worst. What if the overdose had left me with brain damage? I knew there must have been a reason I couldn't speak and was now terrified that I'd done myself permanent damage.

As I started to become desperate I got frightened. I could feel myself starting to panic, and her demeanour changed. She kept telling me to calm down, holding my shoulders gently and pleading with me to listen to her.

So I lay as she told me what had happened. I'd been brought in four days previously. As far as they could tell, I'd taken a massive dose of my epilepsy medication mixed with Paracetamol. They couldn't tell exactly how many tablets I'd taken but estimated based on what James had delivered to me it was around thirty. The reason I couldn't speak or move properly was because of the huge side effects that a dose that big had had.

As she started to tell me, my memories of that horrible night started to flood back and I began to cry. She was kind and looked at me sympathetically. That only made me worse. I still didn't believe I deserved her or anybody else being nice to me and I just wanted to close my eyes and pretend I wasn't there. She told me I was very lucky to be alive and that I was in the best place. As I lay there, trying to fall back asleep, I didn't feel lucky at all.

The next time I came round, it was meal time and the smell had woken me. I was still feeling horrible and couldn't stomach anything so I went without another meal. Of course, they tried to cajole me into eating but the truth was that I had no stomach for food. What I do remember though is that this was the first time I could actually speak and communicate properly, so when I said I wasn't hungry I was pleased with myself for being able to get the words out, albeit slurred. It took me a few tries but I told the nurse I wasn't hungry and didn't think I could stomach anything. I was very thirsty though and so she brought me some water.

Once I'd had a drink, I started to look around the ward. I was still tired and very groggy but I realised it was visiting time. Looking around and seeing all of the other patients with their visitors only made me realise how alone I was. I didn't need another reminder, so I lay down, closed my eyes and cried myself to sleep.

That night I was moved to yet another ward. I presumed that this was because I was now conscious and didn't need as much care.

The new ward was bright and in the morning, the nurses came round and opened all the curtains. I'm sure they do that to make people feel better and brighter but, for me, it just meant I had nowhere to hide. The lady in the bed opposite, noticed me straight away. She was friendly but I wasn't really in the mood for conversation and I wasn't ready for anyone to know my private business, so when she asked what I was doing in hospital, I quickly replied that it was because of my epilepsy. I was still too ashamed to tell anyone the truth.

A little while later a nurse came round to each patient to carry out her observations. When she got to me, she took my blood pressure and pulse and asked how I was feeling. By that time I had some strength and I begged her to take the catheter away so that I could walk to the toilet. She told me that in her opinion it might be too early but that she would remove the catheter if I agreed to have a portable toilet brought to my bedside. That way, I'd have the dignity of going to the toilet alone without the fear of me falling if I tried to walk too far. It was a good compromise and I agreed.

I managed to stand up to prove that I could and true to her word she removed the catheter.

As we were talking, she told me that my husband had phoned to check up on me. As well as being really surprised that James had called, I remember feeling upset. All I wanted to do was to turn back time and change what I'd done but I knew it was too late and I had lost him and the children for good; here was a good man who still cared enough to check up on me. I had thrown him and my life away. I just wanted to be able to erase all of their hurt and take it all back. I had thought that killing myself would have at least given them some peace but it seemed I couldn't even do that properly.

After what I'd done with Chris, James was convinced that our relationship was over for good.

He'd later told me how much my infidelity had hurt him. Of course, our relationship had already hit rock bottom and Social Services were involved in our family. James had decided that he simply didn't want to live like that anymore. He came from a background with strong family values and understandably wanted that for our children too. As far as he was concerned, I was never going to be able to provide that and at this point, our relationship was finished with me out of their lives forever.

Recently I asked him what changed his mind, he honestly replied, it was sympathy. He said it was seeing how pitiful I was when he came to visit me in hospital. My face was all cut up, I couldn't talk and I didn't really know who I was or anything. He said he just thought, "My God, what a sorry state to be in and how did it get to this? That's the mother of my children lying there in that bed."

Lying in the hospital bed, feeling groggy, I didn't really know about the cuts and I couldn't remember taking the overdose but when James saw me, his face showed his shock. I wasn't the girl he'd fallen in love with and married. I was just a shadow of myself.

It was getting close to midday when the nurse came to do my checks, and by then, the ward assistant was bringing round the lunches. I said I wasn't hungry and didn't want anything, but the nurse pointed out that it had been almost seven days since I'd had anything to eat. She told me that I'd probably feel better and stronger if I could force something down. It would also take away a lot of the sickness I was having.

I agreed to try and after half a sandwich and a cup of tea I realised she was right. I did start to feel a little stronger and less sick.

Soon, it was time for the doctors to do their rounds. There were four doctors in total, three male and a female, they took each patient one by one with all four of them discussing the patient and their needs. When they got to my bed, they closed the curtains to give me some privacy.

A male doctor asked how I was feeling first of all. I said that I was feeling better and mentioned that I had managed to have something to eat. After that the female doctor took over. While the first doctors' tone had been kind and gentle, she was much harder. Looking me straight in the eye she said "You are a mother! Why are you letting this addiction, your addiction to alcohol ruin your poor children's lives as well?" She paused for breath and I started to cry. Then she asked me a question I hadn't considered

"How do you think your children would have felt if you had died?"

Up until that point, everyone I had spoken to had been kind and had almost sugar-coated what I was doing there and what would happen to me. Her voice however was totally different. She was harsh and firm and so I did what I always did when my problem was confronted. I sobbed and felt sorry for myself. I convinced myself in those few seconds that she had just taken against me and was being horrible because she could.

She wasn't finished though and she kept asking me how Luke, Liam and Ami would have felt when they were told I had died? How would they have coped with what I'd done?

For the first time I started to listen to her words, there wasn't any getting away this time and there wasn't a bottle I could lose myself in. I started thinking and I knew that I would never forget these words.

Then they told me that a decision had been made about my care. I would be removed from the hospital that had treated the medical conditions my overdose had caused to the Mental Health Care Team. There they would focus on my addiction to alcohol.

As she told me about the plans for my recovery I felt a huge sense of relief. I'd always turned down help when it had been offered but I knew I couldn't carry on as I was. What she had said and the way she had said it had really forced me to think about what I was doing to James, to our friends and family but most of all to our children.

I knew I had an addiction and for the first time in my life I wanted to make it go away.

I knew that I had no choice but to agree and I sobbed quietly as they left. Before she left me alone, the female doctor with the sharp voice took my hand. She squeezed it tightly and said kindly "Emma, you must do this." Then they left me to think.

As far as I'm concerned, my entire outlook changed during that conversation. It was that lady doctor who made me change, she made me sit up and listen.

I know in my heart that if it hadn't been for her then I might be sitting with a drink still in my hand or even dead, but her passion and her determination set off a spark in me that made me want to fight. For once though, I didn't want to fight everyone else. I wanted to fight the demon inside me. I wanted to make it go away permanently. Her passion passed over to me and I will be forever grateful to her for that.

From that moment, I confronted my addiction and our battle

began.

I still think of her from time to time. I wonder what I'd say to her. I probably wouldn't know where to start but I'd let her know that what she said to me that day changed me and the method that she used, the one that finally got through to me, ended up saving my life and my whole family.

On my bad days, I think of her and I feel stronger.

For the longest time ever, I lay and considered what they'd said. A thousand thoughts danced around my head and I actually started to feel like a fighter.

I knew I had to start slowly, so the next time I wanted to go to the toilet, I was determined to walk. I had to try sometime and I hated the thought of using the portable toilet again so I decided to give walking a go and slid gingerly off the bed. I was quite surprised to find that I didn't feel dizzy as I was expecting to.

On the way the nurse kindly asked if I was okay. I nodded and said I would be sure to call her if I needed help. I walked into the bathroom and got the shock of my life: my reflection. I hadn't seen a mirror since I woke up and I couldn't believe what I was seeing. At first, I had to do a double take because I looked so awful, my reflection wasn't me, it wasn't the Emma I knew.

I looked like I had been beaten. My face was covered in scabs and my eyes and cheekbones were covered in huge blue and purple bruises. As I touched one of them, it hurt and I couldn't believe that I could have been there all this time and not realised what a state I was in.

I felt so lost. My body physically ached from the emotional pain and I felt like a small child. I just wanted someone to hold me, to look after me and to tell me that everything would be alright. As I started to cry, I remember feeling so desperate that I wanted to scream.

Then I got angry with myself again and the words from the doctor earlier came back to me. What if I had died? What would have happened to my children then? Luke, Liam and Ami didn't deserve what was happening and the thought of them living without me was horrifying.

She was right. Everyone who had been talking to me for so long to try to get me to face up to what was happening had been right: my children needed me and I needed them. I desperately wanted to be back with my family and with James, even though I had blown things between us.

My thoughts returned to a conversation James and I had a long time ago. His words ringing in my head "We were drinking to have a laugh but you Emma, just used to change. In the end, I'd be saying 'you've got a problem that you need to sort out' until I got fed up of saying it. It just felt like a waste of my breath. It used to go round in vicious circles. We'd argue, I'd tell you to stop or calm down, you wouldn't and I'd forget about it. And we just used to repeat the cycle time and time again. It was never ending. Emma please stop drinking."

I started to think about all the things people were saying to me, from James begging me to get help to the doctor shouting at me to think of my children.

For as long as I could remember I had been wanting my life to end. I'd done so many things to make that happen and yet I kept surviving. If I had died it would have been the most selfish thing I could have done. It would have meant leaving James and the children to clean up my mess. Hurting them was the last thing I had ever wanted to do.

The answer wasn't at the bottom of a bottle and I couldn't keep playing games with my life.

For the first time, the only answer left was to hold my hands up and admit the truth.

I'm an alcoholic and it was ripping my family apart.

And there, as I stood in the bathroom looking at my gruesome face in the mirror, I finally surrendered.

Chapter 23

The following month was the hardest of my life. Without the alcohol to help, I would finally have to admit to my addiction and the damage I had caused. In some ways; that was the scariest thing because the more I found about myself and the things I had done when I was drunk, the more I realised I would have to work hard to put it right.

As I started to put my thoughts together, I realised that the saddest part of the situation was how much I'd hurt James and our children. James, who had been the only person throughout the whole of my adult life, had been truly on my side and who loved me unconditionally, still stood by my side supporting me. Our children deserved so much more from me; their mother.

James visited me in the hospital every day. Most days he would come alone and didn't stay long. He'd had to arrange babysitters and could only stay for an hour or so. It wasn't long but it was enough to give me something to look forward to. On other days he'd bring the children with him but they couldn't understand why I was there and Liam and Ami would get so upset that in the end, it was kinder to them if they stayed at home.

The visits were strange, and it took me a while to get used to them. Firstly there was no privacy for us. James wasn't allowed in my bedroom and although the hospital had lots of space to walk around, there wasn't anywhere I felt we could actually talk. We had a communal garden filled with benches and trees, a lounge where we could sit inside if the weather wasn't too good, but it always seemed like someone was listening.

The staff were watching mine, and the other patients every move. Yet all any of us wanted was a little privacy, so we all crowded to the outdoor areas.

We were allowed to smoke in the grounds but there weren't any matches or lighters permitted inside so the only thing we had was a giant version of a car cigarette lighter. It was attached to the wall and we had to huddle closely to it to light up. Being able to have a smoke calmed my nerves and made it easier to talk through my feelings with James.

Having him there made me feel like I could breathe again. I didn't deserve to have him, yet here he was, still visiting and showing just how much he cared.

One visit in particular really stands out in my mind. The garden was crowded with patients and visitors, all whispering amongst themselves. I was begging James to see how sorry I was and to let me come home with him. I was so upset and couldn't understand why he wasn't seeing how scared I was.

He was very gentle but firm with me and told me that if I didn't let this drop then he would have to go. He was there as a friend and that he had come to support me, not upset me. I simply couldn't calm down though. I was sure that if he could just realise how sorry I was then he would see me in a different light.

After a while, he stuck to his promise and told me he was going home. He would call me the following day.

As soon as he'd left, I began to feel a pain in my chest, like I was being stabbed. Only it wasn't a physical sensation, it was an aching for James. I'd never had to deal with these feelings sober and I honestly didn't know how I'd be able to carry on.

Without a drink to dull these feelings, I was left feeling the full weight of them and I hurt more than I'd ever thought possible.

I couldn't do anything. My first instinct was to find a quiet place and scream until the pain went away but there was nowhere to hide. I was sharing a room so I couldn't go there and if I tried it in any of the public areas I'd be restrained or drugged.

Instead, I went into one of the toilets and closed the door behind me. I didn't scream, but I knew that if I didn't take a few moments alone then I would end up breaking down and I didn't want that either. Of course, my disappearance hadn't gone unnoticed and one of the nurses knocked on the door a few minutes later. She asked if I was okay as I'd been a while. She asked me to open the door and said that if I didn't then she'd have no choice but to open it. All of the doors in the hospital had locks on both the inside and out so that we couldn't lock ourselves in anywhere.

Reluctantly, I did as she asked and opened the door with tears streaming down my face. She took me back to my room and suggested I get some rest before the evening medication rounds.

The next day, James came back again. This time, I knew I couldn't bring up the subject of us being together because of what had happened the day before, but we still had so much to say to each other.

Many of my memories of those days are hazy. Restarting all of my medication for my Bipolar Disorder and my Epilepsy meant that I'd have days I can't even remember and conversations I didn't know I'd had. For this reason, I asked James to help me to piece together what happened during the rest of his visits.

This is what he told me:

"At the time, I found it hard to look at Emma. I loved her so much but how could I forget what she'd done? At the same time, I felt sorry for her every time I looked at her.

I knew how much she loved the children and it was through knowing that, when I realised just how much of a problem she had. She couldn't have hurt the kids the way she did if she'd been able to control her drinking.

I remember asking her what she wanted and where she wanted to go from here. She told me that she wanted to come home. She wanted to be a part of our family and to never drink again. I'd heard her say that a thousand times before and I couldn't bring myself to believe another empty promise.

I was done, and I wasn't going to back down again. Emma really did need to learn the hard way that the drinking could never happen again. I wasn't going to roll over anymore and I wasn't going to forget about what had happened.

Over time though, I started to see a change in her. Every day, a little more strength would appear. I still had my guard up but it was hard not to see the passion she was showing towards her recovery.

As much as I loved her, she wasn't coming back home. As far as I was concerned, she had a long way to go before I could start to forgive, let alone forget. And yet, with each visit, I could see the light returning to her eyes. She was becoming my Emma again.

Physically she was starting to look better. Her face was healing and the cuts and bruises were fading. I could also imagine that she was feeling better not waking up with a hangover every morning.

The day I left her at the hospital upset, it had been about four weeks since she'd last had a drink and I remember thinking it was a record. The longest I'd ever known her to go without a drink for. She was always telling me that she wanted to come home and I was still saying no.

As well as dealing with my own feelings of grief and loss, I had the children to worry about. They weren't coping very well and I was picking up the pieces. Taking them to school every day and seeing them cry and panic as I left was heart breaking. They were so insecure and worried that I wouldn't return. They were so confused and there was no way I was going to let them go through that again.

A few weeks later, Emma was recovering so well that the hospital had let her leave the grounds for a short time to go for a walk. I told her that I would bring the children and meet her at the park just down the road from where she was.

The children were so excited and I couldn't believe the change in her; or in them when they saw her. They played together and I saw how affectionate she was with them. I could see genuine remorse in her and I started to believe that she might have changed.

After that visit, she started seeing the children regularly. One time I sat in the garden and watched as Emma chased the children around, playing Hide & Seek and running among the trees. It was the first time I could remember us being like a proper family, but all too soon it was time to say goodbye again and the children were devastated at having to leave Emma, their mum.

Life at home was difficult, I was either visiting Emma alone or with the children, trying to keep the house running and the children in a routine. It wasn't easy. Luke was old enough to understand and he never gave me any problems at all. He was as good as gold and nothing phased him, but what had happened hit Liam and Ami really hard. They didn't want to go to school and would scream at me not to leave them. Every time I dropped them off, it broke my heart. I would call the school later to check on them and was always told that they'd settled once I'd left but it didn't make me feel any better. Every morning was emotional torture.

The school had a Family Liaison Officer who was a huge help to us. She was always there for a chat. On top of everything, we were struggling financially. I had to give up work suddenly when Emma left, we were entitled to claim for government benefits, but they were taking ages to process and so times were really hard for a while. I told the family liaison officer and she arranged for food parcels from local charities and food banks to be donated to us while we waited.

Peter from Social Services was also coming round to see us. He never stayed very long but we never went more than a few days without him checking on us.

I received a lot of support from my family. My brother, whom Emma had fallen out with, came to visit us for the first time I could remember and the kids loved seeing him.

Every time I visited Emma she told me how much she wanted to come home. By this point, I could see the determination in her and I knew she was telling me the truth. I believed her when she told me she wanted to fight the addiction that had been controlling her.

Still, I was worried. Because everyone had been so supportive of me and the children, I was worried that they'd leave us if I let Emma come home. Then what would I do if she fell again? I'd be alone with the children and nobody to help us. For a long time I was in turmoil.

But one day, and after much soul searching, my love for Emma won.

I told her I was willing to give her one final chance and I asked her to move back in with me and the children."

James friends and family must have thought he was crazy to

give me another chance. I'd proved time and again that I wasn't worth the risk and yet here he was again willing to let me come home. As part of my recovery I asked him what it was about me and about us that made him agree to allow me back home.

"The thing is that deep down I knew what you were like without the drink. You was a different person. It really was a Jekyll and Hyde situation. You were the most fantastic woman in the world when you weren't drunk but when you were drunk you were a totally different character. It wasn't you and I knew that. I did understand that underneath it all there was this lovely girl trying to get out. There was a lovely kind side to you that nobody used to see because the only thing that used to get associated with you was the drunk side. And drunk Emma was horrible. It was the most violent and horrific thing ever. But once you took that out of the equation I knew that there was something worth fighting for.

You're the mother of my kids as well. I always wanted us to be a nice, tight little family like I came from. I understand that the fairytale ending doesn't happen for everyone but for us, I knew there was something that kept us alive. Without the drink you were the loveliest person I'd ever met."

Chapter 24

When James told me I could come home, I was so grateful I could hardly speak. I'd missed the children so much that I felt I was craving them.

There wasn't any declaration of love from James at this time though. He was still being just as stern with me and even though he was telling me what I wanted to hear, it was very clear that this was on his terms. To this day, I'm grateful that he did it this way as it's exactly what I needed from him.

What I felt for him and the children at that time, and what I still feel now is a deep yearning. It's stronger than any craving I ever had for alcohol and although I do wish that I'd changed sooner, I also believe in destiny. Everything happens for a reason and I was supposed to follow the path I did until the very end. I'm just so glad that I found my way home eventually and know that I will never leave it again.

As much as I was desperate to leave the hospital and go home it was a strange feeling.

I remember being really excited when I pulled up outside the house. I stepped out of the car and walked down the path. James hadn't told the children I was coming, so their reactions were amazing. Ami was sitting on the sofa watching TV and as soon as she saw me, she gave me a huge grin then ran up towards me with her arms stretched out. She shouted "Mummy" which made Liam come running in from the kitchen to see what was going on. I got a huge cuddle from him and he kept asking if I was home to stay. When I told him that I was, he started to cry. My heart felt like it would shatter into a million pieces and I promised him again and again that I was home and this was where I was staying. All I wanted now was the four people inside this house, and nothing else.

Luke was still at school and I couldn't wait to see him. I knew I had a lot of making up to do and it would take him a long time to trust me again but this just made me all the more eager to start.

Luke barely spoke to me at first. Like James, he had heard all of my promises before and had no real reason to trust what I was saying. Although I'd started to heal physically, I still had the cuts and bruises and looked terrible. I was having terrible withdrawal symptoms and not surprisingly, Luke left me alone for a lot of the time. He told me later that for the first few weeks I was home he felt very mixed up. As much as he wanted to be excited that I was going to get better, he couldn't let himself believe it.

I was so happy to be home but James still seemed hugely conflicted. He'd always been the strong one and to see him almost beaten by what I'd put him through, and all of the feelings he must have had, was devastating to me. Seeing him like that, as horrid as it was, just made me more determined that I needed to spend every second making it up to them all. They had to see that I had changed and that I was worth this final chance.

There was also a lot to adjust to. James, together with Jenny and Rich had done an amazing job of keeping the house together and looking after the children but there had been some changes to the house and I would need to adapt to them.

They'd bought a few things, like a new rug for the living room and upstairs in "our" bedroom was a wardrobe for

James. I realise that a lot of the things we'd had before had been ruined and James had needed to turn the house into a home for him and the children but it still felt very strange.

There was no room for my clothes in James' wardrobe and I would have to live out of my suitcases for a while. It was like I wasn't a permanent resident. I think, I might have been upset before but I was just so pleased to be home, to be sharing this house with my family again that the negative bits seemed small. I felt lucky to simply be allowed to return to the house and be with my family after what I'd done.

My relationship with Jenny and Rich was ruined though and I knew I had a lot of proving to do. They had seen all the pain I had caused to James and the children and it would take a long time and a huge change on my part before they could forgive me. From a mothers' point of view, I can't blame Jenny at all. Like her, I'm a mother who loves her children and she had seen her son hurt and devastated by what I had put him and her grandchildren through. If she and Rich were angry with me, it was only a reaction to what I had done to James.

The relationship between James and me was also horribly strained. He hardly came near me and although we slept in the same bed he showed no affection. It was like a constant reminder of how much I'd hurt him and how far we had to go. I remember being constantly terrified that this was the end for us and we'd never be able to get past what I had done.

If I'm being honest, I know that this wasn't a healthy way for us to be but I was so scared to talk to James, just in case he changed his mind and decided that I wasn't worth it after all, so I just kept quiet. I would go to bed early because the new medication would knock me out and James would stay up all night. I didn't really know why at the time but now realise that he was so depressed by everything, he couldn't sleep.

I knew that if we couldn't talk then we stood less of a chance of making things work but I just couldn't find the words, so I did the only thing I could which was to give James the time to see how much I'd changed.

The tension in the house must have affected the children too. Gone were the arguments and the furious shouting but we'd just replaced it with a heavy silence and a permanent atmosphere. I hadn't wanted this for them either. I just wanted to give them a normal childhood with a loving and light home to come home to, but it would take time.

Being back at the house just brought me back to the whole situation with Gloria too. With no alcohol to help me, I was too scared to face her and so I felt like a prisoner in my own home: unable to go out in case she saw me. It got to the point where I didn't even want to go into the garden.

My fears affected the children too. I felt very nervous and panicked every time they went to play outside, hovering around the windows just to make sure they were okay but not showing enough of myself that anyone would notice me. Luckily, the children next door had moved away and without them to play with, they seemed happier to be inside, but it didn't change the fact that my behaviour, and my need to stay inside wasn't healthy for them.

It wasn't just Gloria that I didn't want to face, I had shown myself up and made a fool of myself in front of so many people that I didn't want to go out at all.

Thank goodness for Alison. Not only was she the best friend anyone could have, especially through recovery but she and James had become close that she was there for him too. Alison and her husband Kelly would come round a few times a week to see us and make sure James had everything he needed to look after the children, and to look after me. Eventually we started to socialise rather than be looked after and it was their visits that brought James and I back together.

I know that if it hadn't been for them, our relationship simply wouldn't have survived.

At first, Alison just came to visit me but over time, she became a sort-of counsellor for me and James. She'd have us sitting in the kitchen talking about what was going on. We had a lot of emotions and occasionally our discussions would turn heated, but Alison was always there to offer her support and act as a mediator, helping us to have healthy discussions about the past and the future rather than our usual screaming matches.

Slowly, with Alison's help James and I started to be able to enjoy spending time together. We had been living for so long with our guards put up against each other, neither one of us daring to say anything to upset the other; that we'd retreated into ourselves. With her support us we could work on our relationship and start to remember why we were so important to each other in the first place.

Alison was determined that the house shouldn't be quite as gloomy, so we started to watch family films. She and Kelly would come over on a Saturday morning and spend the day with us. We'd have sausage sandwiches and while James and Kelly jammed, we'd chat in the kitchen. Having spent most of my adult life in a houseful of drunk people, as one of them, it was nice to be finally doing normal adult things.

One morning, James had made arrangements to meet Jenny and Rich. They still hadn't forgiven me and wouldn't speak to me, so if James wanted to see his parents he would always go over to them. I was lying on the sofa watching the television when there was a knock at the door. I still got a bit flustered about answering it but I knew I had to test myself a little and I went to answer it. I was shocked to see Jenny and Rich standing on the doorstep.

I went bright red and asked, stammering, if they wanted to

come in. James had been in the kitchen but as soon as he heard his mum's voice he came through. Jenny looked me straight in the eye and said "So, do you promise me Emma that you are never going to drink again and hurt my poor son? He and your children have been through enough now!"

I looked right back at her and told her, with all the strength I had "I promise you with all my heart, I want to beat this, and so yes I promise you."

Jenny threw her arms around me and pulled me into a tight hug. I felt so grateful to her that day. I knew how much it meant to James that she and Rich had come round, and it would mean the world to the children as well. She and Rich had always looked out for me, and gaining their approval again was a huge step in my recovery as well as being massively important for me personally.

As much as I hated her at the time, I also believe Gloria played a huge part in my recovery too. It was her attitude and behaviour towards me that really brought my drinking problems to a head. Without what she did and what I did in response, I could have kept on drinking for years and completely lost my family. I am grateful for her part in my recovery, and although I'll never know why she took against me as much as she did, I'm glad that it happened, because it forced me to change my ways.

Since leaving the hospital I had spent four months in my home. I was severely depressed, and that coupled with not wanting to face anyone through fear meant that I didn't set foot outside.

I was facing everything alone and although I desperately wanted to leave the house, inside I was terrified. I felt after everything I'd done, people would be staring and judging me. I couldn't face it and so I didn't. I had a nurse come to see me every day, she would always try to encourage me to go outside, even if it was just for a few minutes but I was reluctant. One day, I promised her that I would go to the top of the hill. It was only a five minute walk and although I'd agreed, I lost my nerve completely. I started to panic and couldn't breathe properly. I told her that I'd changed my mind and we would try again tomorrow. Six weeks went by and tomorrow never came.

Not being able to leave the house meant I felt constantly guilty. Liam and Ami both had events at school, including their Christmas plays, but I was so terrified about seeing people and having them stare at me that I didn't dare go. I felt like I was letting them down all over again.

After a few months into my sobriety, I sat James down and told him we needed a fresh start. Everyone around us knew what had happened and I felt we would never be able to move on if we stayed there. I was still worried about everyone judging me who knew me when I was drinking. I wanted to put the past behind us and focus on our future.

James agreed that a new start would be the best thing for our family and we sat down to look at the mutual exchange posts again. We found a house about the same size as ours and the lady living there was looking to move to our area. From the photos it looked perfect, I was so excited and it was the fresh start I had been looking for.

One small problem though, the house was about ten miles away in East Malling. It was a lovely town but it would mean moving the children's school again as well and completely uprooting them. The more I thought about the house the more it seemed like the right thing to do. Being that far away from anyone who knew me and my past would give us a completely fresh start. James however wasn't as keen. He was worried about the children and how much they'd already been through. Of course, I was worried about that too but I knew that could be a positive thing for them, as giving me a fresh start would mean that they had one too. I felt it was better for them to be in a place where nobody knew what their Mummy used to be like as well. When I explained this to James, he agreed. After a lengthy discussion, he slowly came round and said there was no harm in looking. I arranged a viewing as soon as possible.

This was the first time I'd left the house in months. We drove through the countryside to get there and although the great outdoors had never really appealed to me, there was something about driving past the fields and through the tunnels made by the trees either side of the road. I relaxed and for the first time in a long time I started to feel calm; like a weight was lifting off me.

We arrived at the house and I could tell that James was impressed. Every room was huge and had been well looked after. There were three good size bedrooms and a lovely garden that was just right for us. Then James saw the huge double shed and his eyes lit up. He started planning there and then what he was going to do with that shed, he talked about building his own music studio just like he'd always wanted. The lady who lived there said that she definitely wanted ours and we made the initial arrangements there and then. Coming home, we were both buzzing with the excitement

We didn't need any more convincing and in February 2012, we moved into our new home.

On the morning of the move, Alison, Jenny and Rich turned up to help us along with a friend of ours, John. As we loaded boxes into the van, I started to feel a little nervous about being outside but I was so excited for our new start that they turned into butterflies of excitement. Knowing that we had the support of our friends and family made it a lot easier to stay strong too. When we arrived at the house, everyone was starving and I remember feeling a hand slip into mine. It was Luke, smiling at me saying "Come on Mum, we'll go for a walk and find some lunch." My eldest son and I walked down the road together happily.

Having Jenny, Rich, Alison and John there to support and help us in our move made me realise just how much I cared for them all. Once I'd only been concerned about me and what I wanted, but now I had this extended family of people looking out for me, James and the children. Over the years, I'd moved to lots of different houses for lots of different reasons, yet none had ever felt as right as this one. I was coming home and I had my family and friends backing me.

Slowly we adjusted to our new way of life in our new home, but it was several weeks before we finally moved the children from their schools. I had been anxious about leaving the house, but things were improving. The cost in fuel alone for the commute each day to and from the school was costly and we needed to move the children to a school closer.

I was willing to go out and had begun to explore the area around our new home, enjoying the freedom that a new beginning was giving me.

James and I sat down to research the several local schools. One was about a fifteen minute walk away and looked perfect. We didn't want to disrupt the children but at the same time, I wanted to be part of their schooling. I was desperate to go to assemblies and parents evenings but didn't dare while they were still in our old area. I wanted us to be a normal family more than ever, I wanted to take them to school and support them.

James knew our new area much better than I did and gave me directions so I could find the school on my daily walks. As I turned the corner to see the new school I got so excited. It was the prettiest building I'd ever seen. It was surrounded by trees and had a huge playing field at the back.

It was so bright and lovely that I could imagine looking

forward to taking Liam and Ami every day.

I walked into reception, introduced myself and explained our situation in full to the receptionist. I never wanted to lie about what had happened in the past. It was part of what and who we were and if the school was going to support Liam and Ami, they would need to know about my drinking.

The lady in reception was lovely. She thanked me for being so open and although I was still expecting some people to be judgemental, she never was. She checked the numbers and said that there was room in the right classes for both Liam and Ami.

On the one hand, I was absolutely thrilled. This seemed like such a lovely school and would be a great environment for them both, but on the other hand they, Liam especially, were settled and happy where they were so I didn't know how we were going to break the news to them. We made arrangements for them to go in for an hour the following week to have a look, sit in their classes and see what they thought and I left to consider the best way to tell them.

As expected, the news didn't go down very well. Ami wasn't happy, while Liam was completely devastated at the thought of leaving all his friends. They both very reluctantly agreed to go and have a look at the new school.

If they had gone in looking and feeling miserable they certainly didn't when they came out. James and I were both thrilled with how well they had settled and they both agreed that they'd be happy to change schools.

Liam, who we had been worried about settling, got some great news. One of his teachers from his old school was actually moving to the new school and would be starting at the same time as him. He'd always loved her so it was brilliant timing.

It wasn't long before they had both settled in their new classes and within weeks they were running into the playground excitedly each morning.

Choosing that school is one of the best decisions we've ever made. The whole environment is so nurturing and full of love. The support they've given to both children and us as a family has been amazing and some of the assemblies they put on are world class for emotion!

Through taking Liam and Ami to school, I've made so many new friends. I feel like part of the community now and am happy being their mum rather than recognised for what I used to be.

It taken time but we've got some really good friends now. Our estate is like a little village; everyone knows everyone and we all look out for each other a completely different contrast to what we were used to.

The move was the best thing we could have done and I honestly don't ever want to live anywhere else. We have good neighbours who look out for us, and who we're happy to look out for, and James' Auntie Val lives just down the road from us. Domestically speaking, we couldn't have been happier.

I was still recovering though and my ongoing sobriety is my biggest achievement to date. Once I'd found the strength to leave the house, I did start to attend some Alcoholics Anonymous meetings. Through those meetings, I learned how people like me manage to live with their illness and seeing how people still managed to live a normal life in spite of that illness was hugely empowering for me.

The biggest thing I noticed at first was the sharing that went on. Alcoholics Anonymous encourages total honesty and because many addicts are used to having to lie in order to get what they need, this honesty is absolutely necessary for recovery. At first, the sharing felt so alien to me that I would just sit and listen. It wasn't that I didn't want to open up more I didn't know how. I'd spent so much of my life lying and hiding to cover my tracks that the idea of being completely transparent was very daunting.

Even so, I was drawing a lot of strength from listening to other people tell their stories and each time I left a meeting I felt that little more empowered. Eventually I started to share my truths as well and although I don't attend meetings religiously, I do make sure I stick to the twelve steps that Alcoholics Anonymous teaches.

One of the major lessons I took from Alcoholics Anonymous was how good it felt to help other people. I'd never set out to be a selfish person but as a drinker, the addiction turned me into a very self-motivated person doing anything for the next bottle. Through sobriety and Alcoholics Anonymous I found that doing good things for others made me immensely happy.

I was also spending a lot of time online during the initial days of my release from hospital. I found social media to be really helpful as there were lots of pages for the newly sober.

Then one day I had a brainwave and decided to create my own group on Facebook. It could have been a completely crazy idea but I thought that if I could share my journey, my bad days and the good then I might make some friends and possibly be able to help people too.

I called my page "Emma Bushen's Journey to Sobriety." It seemed like a fitting name and was the best way I could think of to share my road to sobriety and try to inspire others.

For the first few weeks, the page had a handful of likers and they were all my own friends and family. Then, slowly the numbers started to rise. I'd get the occasional message telling me a story or asking for my advice. People would tell me that my page was helping them and it was truly the best feeling ever.

I was still practising my own sobriety and I was always honest about what I was doing and feeling. It wasn't long before I had people joining my page from all over the world and as thrilled as I was that they trusted me enough to tell me their stories, I started to feel stronger knowing that there were people out there who were just the same as me.

I wasn't alone with my problem anymore and I just wanted to help as much as I could. One thing I've always liked about Alcoholics Anonymous is that it's run by former addicts. That gives them the unique perspective that only an addict has and although I've never claimed to be an expert of any kind, I just wanted to be able to offer support and a friendly ear.

The more I did to help, the more I found I wanted to. In addition to keeping my page running and starting to write my story, I decided I wanted to do something positive for the organisations that help people just like me. I thought if I could just help one charity or organisation I'd be showing how thankful I was for my own sobriety.

So I started to research into the local alcohol charities and found The Kenward Trust. I remembered the name as it was one that the doctors had given me in hospital to contact for my own recovery. Although I hadn't contacted them personally I did start to look at what they did and what I could do to help.

Their services revolve around people who want to address their own issues and make better lives for their families. They help alcoholics like me as well as those with substance abuse problems.

They focus on getting people into residential care and have clinics and counselling sessions. The more I read about them, the more I realised I wished I'd found them earlier, they could have been a huge help to me. Maybe if I'd known about them then I might have sought help earlier or seen that there was a better way for me to be, rather than "Drunk Emma."

I could see how essential they were to our local community and just how much they had to offer. I had to help.

I decided I would put myself to the test for them and planned to do a sponsored parachute jump.

Once I had James and the children on board with the idea, I got in touch with the Trust to tell them about my plans. Richard Chambers became my contact in the fundraising department. He listened to my plans eagerly and seemed very excited.

He invited James and I to go and see the work they do. We spent the day with him, looking at what went on in their residential settings and seeing what the money I was hoping to raise would be going towards. I felt incredibly excited and passionate about what I would be doing and Richards' devotion to the trust was infectious.

Raising the money wasn't easy. Some people used some of their sponsorship money to pay for the jump itself but I didn't want to go down that route so I paid for the plane myself and let all of the money I raised go straight to the Kenward Trust. Richard obviously had a lot more experience in fundraising than I did and he was a huge help. With his guidance I approached the local papers and they agreed to run a story about my jump and the reasons behind it.

I also decided that I wanted to get the children involved in what I was doing. They'd seen so much of the damage I'd caused and although we'd started to make some really positive steps, I wanted them to be proud of me and to see that I was capable of doing something really worthwhile.

So I approached Liam's head teacher, Sue to tell her what I was doing. I'd never been anything other than honest about my past and she'd always been very supportive so I was excited to tell her my plans.

I was hoping she'd let me get all the children involved in a competition where they could put forward a t-shirt design. I would then wear the winning t-shirt on my jump. Sue loved the idea so much that she not only allowed me to speak to the classes and tell them what I was doing but for weeks she gave up her own lunch times to help the children with their designs. The children were so excited. They had lots of questions and I answered them all very honestly. They did some amazing work and even Liam joined in by submitting a design of his own.

Richard agreed to judge the competition for me and when all of the designs were finished, James and I along with the children took them over to the Kenward Trust for Richard to choose his winner.

With Sue' help, we had an assembly at the school so that we could announce a winner. Richard came with me and explained a little about what the Trust does and why it was so important. Then we asked the children to come outside.

Waiting for us was James with Jenny and Rich. They had arranged to release a flock of doves from the school playground to symbolise what I was doing and what it represented. The children counted down and then Rich released the doves into the sky as the children clapped and cheered. They all flew high apart from one particularly stubborn dove who decided that it didn't want to go at the same time as all the other birds and waited a few minutes. The children thought the dove was very funny and we were all in hysterics, but then as it began to fly away, a silence fell over the playground. We watched it soar higher and higher, and slowly the playground broke out into cheers for the reluctant dove.

I've never felt so proud. I used to get a sense of calm and

determination from watching the sea but as I watched that dove begin to fly I felt the same sensation. There was something inside me that I haven't felt before. I felt it again when I did my parachute jump.

Making the leap out of the plane was one of the most terrifying and exhilarating experiences of my life. I raised over four hundred pound for a cause I truly believe in but I proved to myself that I could do anything I set my mind too.

And I've never looked back.

A few words from James

Towards the end of writing my story, I asked James what he would say to someone in his position if he was given the opportunity.

Here is his answer:

This is a really hard question. There is no set answer to this. The only thing that worked with me is being cruel to be kind. I hate saying that because it just sounds crap but in the end that was the only thing that worked for Emma and it wasn't until she'd lost everything; she's lost me, she'd lost her home, and I had custody of the kids and it was only then that she realised that she had a serious problem and that she had to stop it herself.

You know, they have to want to stop and although I never stopped loving Emma, I had to stop loving her or act like I'd stopped loving her to make her realise that she had to stop and she had to sort herself out.

I'm not saying that that's going to work with everyone but certainly that's the thing that worked with Emma, and that's the only thing that solved the problem with her drinking.

Epilogue

Over the last few years since I became sober, I've learned more about life than I ever thought possible. As well as truly knowing myself and what I want, I've learned about other people too.

Throughout my life there have been true people, those who've had my best interests at heart. Rich and Jenny have given James and I so much support even when they had every reason to turn their back on me. My friends Alison and Kelly kept my family together when James and I didn't have the strength to.

There have also been people who were simply no good for me or didn't care. I don't blame them for the problems I had and my addiction wasn't their fault but I don't think they'd want to know me now.

I'm a different person than I was back then. My journey with alcohol started because I didn't have the confidence to be myself but it turned me into a cocky and vulgar person who couldn't see that I was alienating the good people in my life. I know now that the person I was trying to cover up so desperately was actually the kind and decent person that my friends and family could see.

The problem is that when you're living with an addiction you can't see straight. It's only when you come out the other side that you see clearly.

For the first time in my life, I feel driven. I want to do so much more with my life than I ever would have when I was drinking. As well as helping people via my story and my social media page online, I want to make my family as proud as they make me and most importantly I never want to be apart from them again. They are my life and I really couldn't live without them.

When the doctor asked me those difficult questions in hospital, she saved my life because she asked me what my children would think of me. It took almost losing them forever to make me realise what I had and because of that, I had to fight and let them see the strength I had.

Now when I try to answer that question, all I can hope is that they are proud. I want to make them proud and I want them to see that their Mum will carry on fighting for the rest of her life.

When it came to writing this part of my story, I asked Luke what he thought of me now. And he told me;

"Life now is so much calmer now, there are very few arguments and no fights. I have a real family life at last. I'm really close to you and can tell you anything. I'm so proud of you mum and all what you've been through to get to where you are now. You've shown us a clearer future as we don't want to be like you was. I'm too scared to even have a drink as I'm scared of what might happen."

And there we have it..... The real, awful truth of addiction. I have tried throughout this book to tell my story with complete honesty and that in itself hasn't been easy. But finding out that the truth from my friends and family's perspective was an enormous shock to my system. Hearing what Luke and James had to say was simply heart breaking.

Back when I was drinking, I had my fingers in my ears. I only saw the world through my own eyes and it shocks me that my life then is so far removed from what I could see.

James, Luke, Liam and Ami had every right to give up on me forever and I feel proud and privileged every day that they are still by my side.

My story shows that anybody can have an addiction, but that doesn't need to be the end of their story. There is always hope and there is always redemption, and anyone can find it.

If you are reading this and you are suffering, I want you to know that there is a better life waiting for you. Don't settle for anything less.

Emma xx

Lightning Source UK Ltd.
Milton Keynes UK
UKOW07f1849230215

246765UK00005B/344/P